The DOG Friendly HOME

DIY Projects for Dog Lovers
by Ruth Strother

Creative Publishing
international

MINNEAPOLIS, MINNESOTA
www.creativepub.com

Creative Publishing
international

Copyright © 2011
Creative Publishing international, Inc.
400 First Avenue North, Suite 300
Minneapolis, Minnesota 55401
1-800-328-0590
www.creativepub.com
All rights reserved

Printed in China

10 9 8 7 6 5 4 3 2 1

Library of Congress Cataloging-in-Publication Data

Strother, Ruth.
   The Dog Friendly Home : DIY Projects for Dog Lovers / By
Ruth Strother.
      pages cm
   Includes index.
   Summary: "Instructions and photos for do-it-yourself projects
to build for a dog. Includes information on training, safety and
grooming"--Provided by publisher.
   ISBN-13: 978-1-58923-566-3 (soft cover)
   ISBN-10: 1-58923-566-5 (soft cover)
   1. Dogs--Equipment and supplies. I. Title.
   SF427.15.S77 2011
   636.7'0887--dc22

                      2010042077

The Dog-Friendly Home: DIY Projects for Dog Lovers
Created by: **The Editors of Creative Publishing international, Inc.**

President/CEO: Ken Fund

Home Improvement Group

Publisher: Bryan Trandem
Managing Editor: Tracy Stanley
Senior Editor: Mark Johanson

Creative Director: Michele Lanci-Altomare
Art Direction/Design: Jon Simpson, Brad Springer, James Kegley
Page Layout Artist: Heather Parlato

Staff Photographer: Joel Schnell
Set Builder: James Parmeter
Shop Help: Charles Boldt

Author: Ruth Strother
Contributing Writer: Philip Schmidt
Tech Editor: Eric Smith
Proofreader: Drew Siqveland
Editorial Intern: John Buckeye

Production Managers: Laura Hokkanen, Linda Halls

CONTENTS

14

Introduction 5
Building Materials for Your Pet Projects 6

DOGHOUSES 11
Custom Dog Castle 14
Basic Ranch Doghouse 20
Insulated Doghouse 26
Green Doghouse 34

DOG BEDS 45
Contemporary Dog Bed 48
Nightstand/Bed 54
Mission-Style Dog Bed 60

DOG TRAINING 67
A-Frame 70
Hoop Jump 72
Weave Poles 74
Invisible Fence 76

ACCESSORIES 85
Raised Dog Bowls 86
Dog Ramp 92
Dog Door 98
Toy Chest 102
Grooming Station 108

HOME & YARD 115
Creating a Dog-Friendly Yard 116
Dog Damage Remedies 122

Resources/credits 126
Index 127

48

70

108

120

Introduction

Most of us consider ourselves to be dog lovers. We care for our dogs by walking them, playing with them, teaching them, feeding them, loving them—but we want to do more. The dog-friendly projects in this book were created for beginning do-it-yourselfers who want to make something special for their canine pals. In most cases, all you'll need are a few basic tools and your creativity. These projects are simple, useful, and attractive. If you don't consider yourself to be especially handy with a hammer, saw, or drill, you can get a leg up (pardon the pun) by taking a weekend course offered at many local home improvement stores. You will find the brief introduction on materials and tools that follows to be helpful as well.

This book is filled with tips on dog behavior, care, training, and fun. Each project is accompanied by valuable information that will help you acclimate your dog to its use, happily and without fear. You'll learn not only how to install a dog door, but also how to train your dog to use it. Tips on how to get a reluctant dog to accept and use a bed accompany information about the three styles of bed you can choose from when you build your dog a special place. Included are dietary information to help you fill the raised bowls you just built, and information on grooming accompanied by instructions on setting up your own grooming station—all this and more will help you develop a dog-friendly home.

The information in this book spills out of the house and into the yard as well. You can install an invisible fence and teach your dog how to obey it, and create an agility course in your very own backyard.

In addition, this book will identify toxic plants, offer you tips on how to care for a garden in a dog-patrolled yard, and give you pointers on ways to erase those dog-created brown spots in your lawn. Back inside the home, brief and effective ways to repair dog-chewed furniture and remove soiling accidents are covered.

All the projects in this book were designed with cost in mind. Less expensive materials are used when they don't compromise the quality of the project, and more expensive materials are suggested when they will greatly enhance the beauty and integrity of the project.

Making accoutrements for your dog is a great creative outlet. You can take the structural fundamentals of most of these plans and embellish them with your own designs, colors, and materials to make them especially suited to your dog and the style of your home. Turn the ordinary to the fanciful or dignify the piece with sophisticated style; whatever you decide to do, by building and designing that special something for your canine companion, you are taking that one extra step to do more for your dog and show him how much he means to you.

Building Materials for Your Pet Projects

Building homes and accessories for your pets can be accomplished with many of the same tools and building materials we use in our houses and landscapes. However, in some cases the fact that our pets are more inclined than our children to eat their house does impact the selection process. As with people-scale projects, you'll select materials for your pet projects based on safety, ease of use, appearance, durability, and cost. And most of the projects in this book can be constructed with simple hand and power tools that you probably own already. On the following pages we review some common materials with these considerations in mind. After that, you'll find a very brief refresher course on a few basic woodworking skills you'll need for even the most simple pet projects. Then, we jump feet-first into the pool of pet projects.

Sheet Goods

Sheet goods such as plywood and medium density fiberboard (MDF) can be shaped easily with a router and feature a smooth surface that takes paint well on both faces and edges. Machining most sheet goods produces hazardous dust that needs to be collected.

Interior plywood. Frequently sold with a smooth, finish-grade hardwood veneer surface, plywood may be painted or sealed and stained. Plywood cuts easily and is the easiest sheet good to fasten. Hardwood plywood is expensive and should be sealed to protect it and to slow off-gassing of formaldehyde.

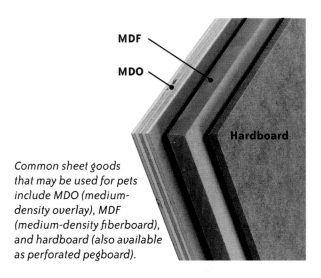

Common sheet goods that may be used for pets include MDO (medium-density overlay), MDF (medium-density fiberboard), and hardboard (also available as perforated pegboard).

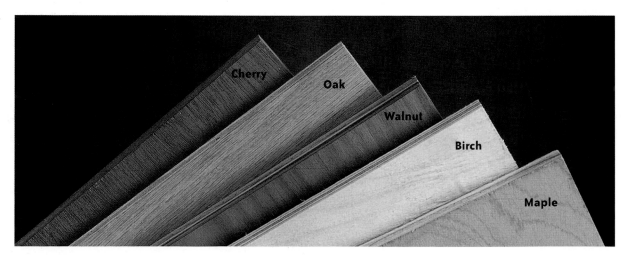

Veneer plywood offers a variety of wood species in a durable and cost-effective panel.

Exterior plywood. Panels are inexpensive and easy to fasten and cut. Exterior plywood does not contain formaldehyde, making it preferable to hardwood plywood for interior structures where appearance is not an issue. Surfaces and edges are rough, and the plywood may not lie flat without framing.

Wood

Softwood construction lumber. Stud grade 2 × 4s, 2 × 2 furring strips, lath, and construction grade 1 × 3s are a few examples of construction lumber that is safe, natural, easy to work with and extremely inexpensive. With a little care, you can turn these rough-and-tumble materials into dog projects that belie their blue-collar pedigree.

Cedar and redwood are naturally rot and insect resistant and hold paint well. Use them for outdoor pet structures. You can find them in the fencing and decking sections of home improvement stores. Do not use cedar shavings, or any wood shavings for that matter, as bedding in doghouses because it can become moldy.

Hardwood. Hardwood is useful for any interior building project, either for making the entire project or to trim out a larger project made with sheet goods or softwood.

Pressure-treated wood. Pressure-treated wood no longer contains arsenic, as it once did, so it's not as toxic as it used to be. Use it on outdoor structures where proximity to soil may cause rot in untreated wood. Avoid pressure-treated wood on parts of structures that may be chewed by your dog.

Miscellaneous Materials

Paints, finishes, chemicals. Find paints, finishes, and chemicals that are nontoxic to dogs with an internet search for "pet safe paint" or "non-toxic paint." These are just two searches of many that you can conduct on the Internet in your quest for paints and chemicals that are safe for your dog.

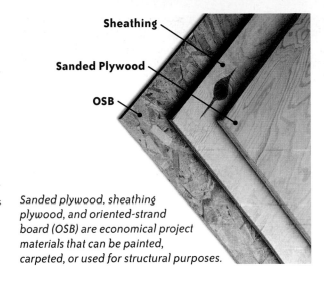

Sanded plywood, sheathing plywood, and oriented-strand board (OSB) are economical project materials that can be painted, carpeted, or used for structural purposes.

Species of lumber that are suitable for pet projects include (clockwise from top): Redwood, pine, maple, oak, poplar, dimensional framing lumber (spruce, pine or fir), and cedar.

Water-base or acrylic paints are safest for use around pets, but whichever finish materials you choose, read the product information very carefully.

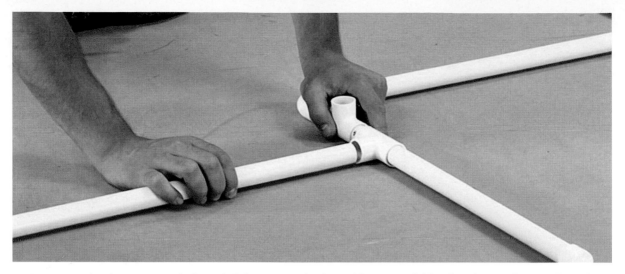

PVC water supply tubing comes in ½, ¾, and 1" diameter, with a host of fittings available. The tubes can be joined together with simple friction, or they can be solvent-welded for permanent connections.

PVC pipe. Polyvinyl chloride (PVC) is easy to use, inexpensive, versatile, and paintable if you scuff it up with sandpaper first. To cut PVC use a miter saw or PVC saw.

Woodworking Techniques

Cutting. Circular saws and jigsaws cut wood as the blade passes up through the material, which can cause splintering or chipping on the top face of the wood when cutting against the grain. For this reason, always cut with your workpiece face down.

To ensure a straight cut with a circular saw, clamp a straightedge to your workpiece to guide the base of the saw as you cut.

A power miter saw is the best tool for making straight or angled cuts on narrow boards and trim pieces. This saw is especially helpful for cutting hardwood. An alternative is to use an inexpensive hand miter box fitted with a backsaw.

Shaping. A belt sander makes short work of sanding tasks and is also a powerful shaping tool. Mounting a belt sander to your workbench allows you to move and shape the workpiece freely using both hands. Secure the sander by clamping the tool casing in a benchtop vise or with large hand screws or C-clamps. Clamp a scrap board to your bench to use as a platform, keeping the workpiece square and level with the sanding belt.

Always use a straightedge cutting guide when trimming panels with a power saw.

To ensure that matching pieces have an identical shape, clamp them together before shaping. This technique is known as gang sanding.

Squaring a Frame is an important technique in furniture construction. A frame or assembly that is not square will result in a piece that teeters on two legs or won't stand up straight. Always check an assembly for square before fastening the parts together.

To square a frame, measure diagonally from corner to corner. When the measurements are equal, the frame is square. Adjust the frame by applying inward pressure to diagonally opposite corners. A framing square or a combination square can also be used to see if two pieces form a right angle.

Piloting and Drilling. Pilot holes make it easier to drive screws or nails into a workpiece without splitting the wood. If you find that your screws are still difficult to drive or that the wood splits, switch to a larger diameter bit. If the screws are not holding well or are stripping the drill holes, use a smaller bit to drill subsequent holes. Use a standard straight bit when drilling pilot holes for finish nails.

A combination pilot bit drills pilot holes for the threaded and unthreaded sections of a screw shank, as well as a counterbore recess that allows the screw to seat below the surface of the workpiece. The counterbore portion of the bit drills a ⅜-inch diagonal hole to accept a standard wood plug. A bit stop with a setscrew allows you to adjust the drilling depth.

When drilling a hole through a workpiece, clamp a scrap board to the back of the piece where the drill bit will exit. This backer board will prevent the bit from splintering the wood.

To make perfectly straight or uniform holes, mount your drill to a portable drill stand. The stand can be adjusted for drilling to a specific depth and angle.

Gluing. For gluing, surfaces should be smooth and free of dust but not sanded. Glue and fasten boards soon after they are cut—machined surfaces, which dry out over time, bond best when they are freshly cut.

Before gluing, test-fit the pieces to ensure a proper fit. Then clean the mating edges with a clean, dry cloth to remove dust.

Apply glue to both surfaces and spread it evenly using a brush or glue roller. Use enough glue to cover the area with a small amount of excess.

Promptly assemble and clamp the pieces with enough clamps to apply even pressure to the joint. Watch the glue oozing from the joint to gauge the distribution of pressure. Excessive squeeze-out indicates that there is too much glue. Wipe away excess glue with a damp—not wet—cloth.

Prepping Wood for Finishing Touches. Some projects require that nail heads be set below the surface of the wood using a nail set. Choose a nail set with a point slightly smaller than the nail head.

Screws that have been driven well below the surface (about ¼ inch) can be hidden by filling the counterbores with glued wood plugs. Tap the plug into place with a wood mallet or a hammer and scrap block leaving the plug just above the surface. Then sand the plug smooth with the surrounding surface.

If desired, fill nail holes and small defects with wood putty. When applying a stain or clear finish to a project, use a tinted putty to match the wood. Avoid smearing it outside the nail holes. Use putty to fill screw holes on painted projects.

A power drill with a sanding drum attachment helps you sand contoured surfaces until smooth.

Use a random orbit or palm sander to finish-sand flat surfaces. To avoid sanding through thin veneers, draw light pencil marks on the surface and sand just until the marks disappear.

A block of wood wrapped in 150-grit sandpaper is used to "break" the edges of freshly-cut wood and panels.

Doghouses

Dᴏɢʜᴏᴜsᴇs ᴀʀᴇ ɴᴏᴛ ᴀ ᴍᴜsᴛ-ʜᴀᴠᴇ ɪɴ ᴇᴠᴇʀʏ ʜᴏᴍᴇ. ʙᴜᴛ ɪғ ʏᴏᴜʀ
ᴅᴏɢ sᴘᴇɴᴅs ᴀ ʟᴏᴛ ᴏғ ᴛɪᴍᴇ ᴏᴜᴛsɪᴅᴇ, sʜᴇ ᴍᴀʏ ᴀᴘᴘʀᴇᴄɪᴀᴛᴇ ᴀ ʀᴇғᴜɢᴇ
from the elements. And, really, that's the main purpose of a doghouse: to keep your pooch dry
and comfortable.

Shelter from the Storm—and the Sun

The elements can wreak havoc with a dog. In warm climates, dogs left outside all day long
without any shelter can get sunburned and become blind from overexposure to the sun. Shade
and water must always be available. It's best to place the doghouse in the shade even if you live
in a mild or cold climate. A doghouse can heat up to dangerous temperatures when exposed to
the sun even if the ambient temperature isn't that high. In colder climates, protection from wind
and cold are paramount. And it helps if the doghouse is raised a few inches off the ground to
help it stay dry.

Sizing Your Doghouse

You certainly don't want your doghouse to be too small, but it's just as important for it not to
be too large—especially if you live in a cold climate. A dog emits body heat, thereby warming
the area around her. But if the doghouse is too big, this warming effect is lost. An easy way to

determine the proper size for your doghouse is to measure a rectangle around your sleeping dog and add three inches in all directions. Then add about six inches to the height of your dog's shoulders to determine a good height for her doghouse. For more detailed information about sizing your doghouse, see the Minimum/Maximum Sizing sidebar on page 29.

Even if you live in a cold climate, don't overheat the doghouse. A dog's fur is a great warm winter coat. Air is trapped in pockets within hair shafts, resulting in good insulation even for shorthaired dogs. Longhaired dogs have a double coat with insulating air pockets. These insulators protect a dog from heat as well as from cold.

Building Don'ts

One of the biggest errors people make when designing or constructing a doghouse is to make it as airtight as possible. It's true a doghouse needs to be sealed well enough to keep the elements out. But without allowing for air circulation, you're creating a friendly environment for molds and germs. The last thing you want to do is create a toxic environment for your dog.

Insulation can pose another potential danger to your dog if it becomes exposed. Some dogs will eat nearly anything, either out of boredom or because they have an insatiable appetite. Insulation can form a blockage in a dog's stomach, which could lead to the dog's death if not caught in time. Instead of using insulation, consider constructing your doghouse with double walls. The doghouse will be insulated by the air trapped between the two walls. If insulation is a must-have in your climate, opt for insulation board, which is a bit safer.

Embellishments

No matter which of the following doghouse plans you choose for your dog, you can add your own personal touch. Don't be afraid to paint, carve, stencil, or otherwise embellish your doghouse to suit your dog's personality.

Bedding

The best bedding for your dog is a collection of old, used blankets. They're easy to clean and don't cost a lot of money. Plus dogs love them, often playing with the blankets more than sleeping on them. Stay away from wood shavings, hay, or straw, which tend to harbor pests, germs, and mold.

Training

Many dogs will curiously investigate a doghouse when first presented with one, but some may be more reticent. There are steps you can take to introduce your dog to her new digs. Make training sessions brief and fun. It's not unusual for a dog to take a few days or even weeks to accept her doghouse.

Take your dog's favorite toy and put it in the doghouse. If your dog is still hesitant to go in, take some food treats that your dog loves, starting a foot or so out from the entrance, and make a Hansel-and-Gretel trail well into the depths of the house. If your dog isn't enticed to follow this trail, start tossing in even tastier food treats. Do this for just a few minutes at a time. Remember, don't push your dog. The doghouse must be seen as a wonderful place by your dog, not one that she's forced to accept.

Custom Dog Castle

Many of us treat our dogs like royalty, so why not provide them with the properly regal abode? This dog castle
will finally prove that Princess really does deserve that tiara she's been sporting since her last trip to the doggy spa.
Of course, this doghouse requires a few more steps than those built for the peons, but it will be well worth it!

Tools, Materials & Cutting List

- Measuring tape
- Circular saw
- Straightedge guide
- Speed square
- Clamps
- Drill with countersink piloting bit and ⅜" twist bit
- Jigsaw
- Level
- Hammer
- Caulking gun
- ¾" × 4 × 8-ft. plywood (2 ½" sheets)

- Finish nail
- (1) 1 × 2" × 8 ft.
- (1) 2" × 2 × 8 ft.
- Waterproof wood glue
- Deck screws (1¼, 1⅝")
- Construction adhesive
- Masking tape
- Paintable exterior caulk
- Painting supplies

Key	Part	Dimension	Pcs.	Material
A	Base	¾ × 44 × 44"	1	Plywood
B	Box front/back	¾ × 30 × 36"	2	Plywood
C	Box side	¾ × 30 × 34½"	2	Plywood
D	Box roof	¾ × 34½ × 34⁹⁄₁₆"	1	Plywood
E	Roof Ledger	¾ × 1½ × 32½"	2	1 × 2
F	Tower wall f/b	¾ × 6 × 14½"	2	Plywood
G	Tower wall side	¾ × 4½ × 14½"	2	Plywood
H	Box corner	¾ × 6 × 34"	8	Plywood
I	Side nailer	1½ × 1½ × 34"	2	2 × 2
J	Front nailer	1½ × 1½ × 8"	2	2 × 2
K	Rear nailer	1½ × 1½ × 33"	1	2 × 2
L	Tower lid	¾ × 6 × 6"	1	2 × 2
M	Tower lid handle	1½ × 1½ × 1½"	1	Plywood

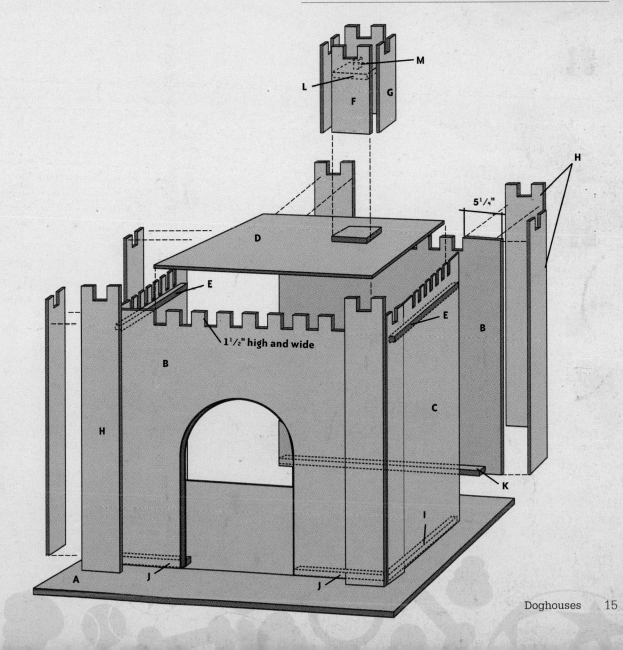

How to Build the Custom Dog Castle

Make a 3° bevel cut at the front edge of the lightly sloping roof panel so the edge fits flush against the back panel. Use a circular saw and a straightedge guide to make the cut.

Cut 1½ × 1½" notches in the tops of the panels to create the iconic crenellation profiles we associate with castle walls. Place a backer board behind the workpiece before drilling access holes for the jigsaw blade.

CUT THE BASE AND BOX PANELS

Cut the base (A) to size at 44 × 44" using a circular saw and straightedge guide to ensure straight cuts. Cut the two side panels (C) to size at 30" high × 34½" wide. Cut the front and back panels (B) at 30" high × 36" wide. Tip: To make your castle smaller or larger than the project as shown here, subtract or add the same amount from each of the given dimensions; note that the box sides, front, and back are all the same height, and the side panels are 1½" narrower than the front and back panels.

Mark the roof panel (D) for cutting at 34½" (side to side) × 34⁹⁄₁₆" (front-to-back). To make the cut for the front edge of the panel, set your circular saw at 3° angle (instead of 0°, which would make a straight 90° cut) to account for the slight backwards slope of the roof (See photo 1). Make the cuts for the back and sides of the panel with the saw set for a straight perpendicular cut.

NOTCH THE BOX PANELS

The squared off, scalloped profiles at the top edges of the panels and towers are known as crenellation details. They feature 1½" square cutouts. You can save time by ganging two panels together and cutting through both pieces at once.

Make a mark on the top edge of the front panel, 5¼" in from each side edge, then mark at 1½" intervals in between. Draw a line 1½" down from and parallel to the top edge. Use a speed square or combination square to draw straight lines from the top edge to the 1½" line at each mark. Label every other square space with an X to designate the squares that will be cut out. Both wide outside squares should be cutouts.

Repeat the process on one of the side panels, but make the first two marks 4½" from the side edges of the panel.

Clamp the front and back panels together so all edges are flush, and include a scrap board behind the back panel to serve as a backer board to minimize tearout. Drill an access hole at the bottom corners of each cutout square, using a drill bit that's slightly larger than the width of your jigsaw's blade. Make sure access holes are drilled in the waste areas only. Cut out the squares to create the crenellations, using a jigsaw (See photo 2). Repeat the same process to make the side-panel cutouts.

MARK AND CUT THE DOOR

Mark a centerline on the front panel, 18" in from each side edge. Use the centerline to mark the desired width of the door cutout. As a general rule, the door should be at least 1" wider than the widest part of your dog. The door height should be equal to at least 75 percent of your dog's height—measured from the ground to the top of the shoulders. As shown, the door opening is 12" wide and 18" high.

To mark the rounded top of the door, measure down half the door width from the top mark, and make a mark on the centerline. Set a compass (or create a shop-made trammel-style compass with a stick and a nail) to equal this radius. Position the compass point (or nail) on the centerline mark, and draw the arch from one side of the door to the other (See photo 3).

Complete the door cutout with a jigsaw. Sand the cut edges to prevent splintering.

ASSEMBLE THE BOX AND BASE

The roof panel is supported by a pair of 1 × 2 ledger boards attached to the inside surfaces of the side walls. Mark layout lines for the ledgers onto the inside faces of the side panels: measure down 2½" from the top of the side panel, and make a mark near the front edge. Make a mark near the back edge, 3½" from the top. Draw a straight line between the marks to create a sloped reference for the ledgers.

Position each ledger with its top edge on the layout line and its ends 1" from the front and back edges of the side panel. Fasten the ledgers with exterior-rated wood glue and 1¼" deck screws driven into the side panels.

Fit the front and back panels over the ends of the side panels so all outer edges are flush, and fasten them together with exterior glue and 1⅝" deck screws driven through countersunk pilot holes.

Set the box over the base so it is centered side-to-side and front-to-back. Make sure the box is square by measuring diagonally between opposing corners: the box is square when the measurements are equal. Outline the box onto the base and then remove it and install nailers (I, J, K) around the inside perimeter of the outline. Set the box back onto the base and screw the bottoms of the panels to the nailers (See photo 4).

Plot an arch at the top of the door cutout with a trammel made from a short length of 1 x 2 with a finish nail driven through at the centerline mark.

Secure the box to the plywood base with screws driven through the box panels and into 2 x 2 nailers.

Back panel

Drill ⅜"-dia. drainage holes at the joint where the back panel meets the roof panel.

Create four corner towers by fastening pairs of 6 × 34" plywood strips at each corner. Cut crenellation notches in the tops of the strips first.

INSTALL THE ROOF

Set the roof panel onto the ledgers so the point of the beveled edge of the roof is touching the front panel. The roof should fit snugly on all sides; if there are gaps, split the difference between opposing sides to make each gap as small as possible.

Fasten the roof panel to the ledgers with 1⅝" deck screws driven through countersunk pilot holes.

Make marks for drainage holes along the corner where the roof meets the back panel, spacing the holes 2" apart. Drill ⅜"-dia. holes through the back panel, angling the holes downward slightly (See photo 5). Drill slowly with light pressure to minimize tearout on the panel faces. Note: If your dog castle will not be exposed to the elements, you can omit the drainage holes.

INSTALL THE CORNER TOWERS

Each of the corners of the doghouse is appointed with a pair of corner boards that meet to form a tower shape. Cut the eight box corners (G) to width and length from plywood and then make a 1½ × 1½ crenellation notch in the top of each board. Attach the boards to each corner with the front and back boards overlapping the edges of the side boards in a neat seam (See photo 6).

MAKE & INSTALL THE TOWER

The centerpiece of this dog castle is a hollow tower structure in the middle of the roof. Fitted with a removable cover, the tower can be used to store a leash, toys, or other dog care supplies. To make the tower, cut two plywood strips to 7½ × 14½" (F) and cut two to 6 × 14½" (G) . Fashion the strips Into a rectangular column with the front and back strips covering the edges of the side strips. Use glue and deck screws driven into countersunk pilot holes. Once the rectangular column is securely assembled, plot out and cut crenellation notches that align.

Next, cut a 6 × 6" lid and fasten a 1½"-long piece of 2 × 2 to the top for a handle. Tack thin wood strips around the inside of the box, ¾" down from the bottoms of the notches. These strips function as lid supports.

Finally, cut a wood block the same size as the lid and attach it to the roof. The tower assembly is then fastened to the block with countersunk screws (See photo 7).

CAULK AND PAINT THE CASTLE

Sand all wood surfaces thoroughly with progressively finer sandpaper until you reach 150-grit sandpaper. For best appearance, fill any voids in the plywood edges and cover all screwheads with waterproof wood filler. Sand the filler smooth after it dries.

Paint the castle as desired, using quality exterior trim paint. Apply two or more coats for weather protection. Let the paint dry completely between coats to ensure proper adhesion. The doghouse seen in the photo on page 14 was painted with primer and then topcoated with a spray-on granite tone.

Seal all exposed joints on the castle with quality exterior caulk (See photo 8). If you apply the caulk after painting, choose a caulk that matches the paint tone.

Fasten the tower to a wood block mounted on the doghouse roof. Orient the tower so the exposed edge grain faces the sides, not the front.

Fill the gaps between panels with caulk. Here, the white caulk is being applied to the primed doghouse prior to the application of the decorative paint.

Basic Ranch Doghouse

The first image that comes to mind when most people think of a doghouse is that of a cube with a roof on it. This ranch doghouse offers more: a sheltered porch and rounded feet to raise it off the ground. A dog can rest on the porch and watch all the goings-on around her while still enjoying some protection from the elements; the raised feet keep the interior of the doghouse dry. This doghouse has a main area with plenty of room for a dog about 15" tall. See the sidebar Minimum/Maximum Sizing on page 29 to determine how big to make your ranch doghouse, then adjust dimensions accordingly. Just imagine your dog hanging out on her very own porch while you garden or toss a ball with your children. What an idyllic scene!

Tools, Materials & Cutting List

- Compass
- Jigsaw
- Power sander
- Circular saw
- Straightedge
- Combination square
- Miter saw (or miter box)
- Backsaw
- Tin snips or aviator snips
- 2" and 3" deck screws
- 6d galvanized finish nails
- Silicone caulk

- Roofing nails with rubber washers
- (2) 1 × 2" × 8' cedar
- (3) 2 × 2" × 8' pine
- (2) 2 × 4" × 8' cedar
- (2) ⅝" × 4 × 8' siding
- (1) ¾" × 4 × 8' exterior plywood
- Sandpaper
- Primer
- Paint
- Paintbrush
- Metal flashing
- Emery paper

Key	Part	Dimension	Pcs.	Material
A	Frame side	1½ × 3½ × 45"	2	Cedar
B	Frame end	1½ × 3½ × 22⅞"	2	Cedar
C	Feet	1½ × 3½ × 7½"	4	Cedar
D	Floor	¾ × 22⅞ × 48"	1	Exterior ply
E	Side panel	⅝ × 30 × 48"	2	Siding
F	House end panel	⅝ × 18 × 24"	1	Siding
G	Porch end panel	⅝ × 24 × 24"	1	Siding
H	Center panel	⅝ × 22⅞ × 23¾"	1	Siding
I	House roof	¾ × 25½ × 35"	1	Exterior ply
J	Porch roof	¾ × 25½ × 23"	1	Exterior ply
K	Side roof trim	⅞ × 1½ × *"	4	Cedar
L	End roof trim	⅞ × 1½ × 27¼"	2	Cedar
M	Flashing	1⁄16 × 4 × 27¼"	1	Galv. flash
N	Cleat	1½ × 1½ × *"	10	Pine

* Cut to fit

OVERALL SIZE:
30" HIGH
27¼" WIDE
48" LONG

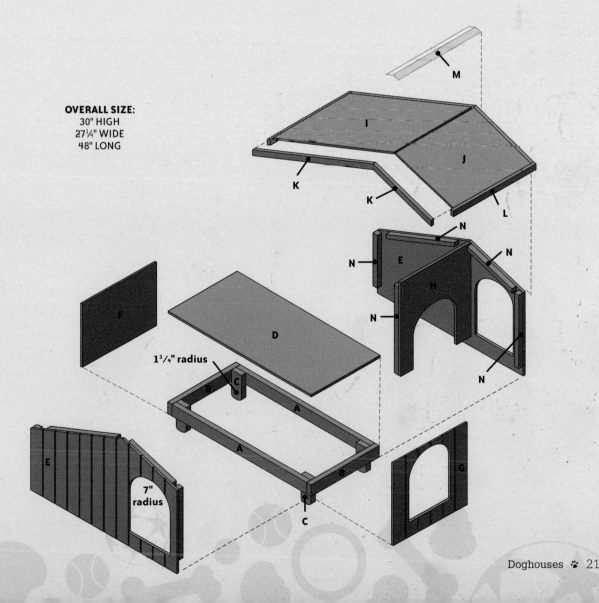

How to Build a Ranch Doghouse

1

Fasten the 2 × 4 cedar feet to the inside frame corners with 3" galvanized deck screws.

2

Lay out the roof angle on the side panels using a straightedge.

BUILD THE FRAME & FLOOR

The frame of the doghouse is the foundation for the floor, sides, and roof. It is built from 2 × 4 cedar lumber.

Cut the frame sides and frame ends to length. Place the frame sides between the frame ends to form a rectangle; then fasten together with 3" deck screws. Make sure to keep the outside edges flush.

Cut the feet to length. Use a compass to lay out a 1¾"-radius roundover curve on one end of each foot, then cut with a jigsaw to form the roundover. Smooth out the jigsaw cuts with a power sander.

Fasten a foot in each corner of the frame with 3" deck screws (photo 1). Be sure to keep the top edges of the feet flush with the top edges of the frame. Angle screws slightly so they don't poke through.

Cut the floor to size from ¾"-thick exterior plywood, and fasten it to the top of the frame with 2" deck screws. The edges of the floor should be flush with the outside edges of the frame.

MAKE THE WALLS

The walls for the doghouse are cut from ⅝"-thick siding panels—we chose panels with grooves cut every 4" for a more decorative effect.

Cut the side panels to the full size listed in the Cutting List on page 21.

Create the roof line by cutting peaks on the top of the panels. To make the cuts, first mark points 18" up from the bottom on one end, and 24" up from the bottom on the

Siding Faces

Most siding products, whether they are sheet goods or lap siding boards, have a front and back face. In most cases, it is very easy to tell which face is meant to be exposed, but you always should be careful not to confuse the two.

Lay out the opening archway on the side panels, using a ruler and pencil.

Cut out the openings in the panels with a jigsaw.

other end. Measure in along the top edge 30" out from the end with the 24" mark, and mark a point to indicate the peak of the roof. Connect the peak mark to the marks on the ends with straight lines to create the cutting lines (photo 2). Lay the side panels on top of one another, fastening them with a screw or two in the waste area. Then, cut both panels at the same time, using a circular saw or jigsaw, and straightedge cutting guide.

Make the arched cutouts in the front (taller) sections of the side panels, by first measuring and marking a point 2" and 16" in from the 24"-tall end of one panel, then drawing lines from the bottom to the top of the panel, through the points. Measure up 4¼" and 15¾" from the bottom edge and draw horizontal lines to complete the square. Find the center point between the sides of the square cutout outline, and measure down 7" from the top of the cutout at that point.

Press down on the end of a ruler so it pivots at that point, and use the ruler and a pencil like a compass to draw a curve with a 7" radius across the top of the cutout (photo 3).

Drill a starter hole at a corner of the cutout outline, then cut the opening with a jigsaw (photo 4). Trace the cutout onto the other side panel, and then make that cutout.

Cut the center panel and porch end panel to full size. Use one of the side panel cutouts to trace an arched cutout outline onto the porch end panel so the sides are 4½" from each side edge and the top is 15¾" up from the bottom. Mark an arched cutout outline on the center panel, 3⅞" from each side edge and 15¾" up from the bottom.

Make the cutouts with a jigsaw, and then sand all cut edges smooth.

Fasten the center panel by driving screws through the side panels into the cleats. Use a combination square to keep the panel even.

Cut each side roof trim piece to fit between the peak and the end of the roof panel, mitering the ends so they will be perpendicular when installed. Attach all the roof trim pieces with galvanized finish nails.

ATTACH THE WALLS & FRAME

Cut the house end panel. Fasten the side panels to the frame with 2" deck screws, so the bottoms of the panels are flush with the bottoms of the frame, and the ends of the panels are flush with the frame ends.

Fasten the house end panel and the porch end panel to the frame so the bottoms of the panels are flush with the bottom of the frame (the sides of the end panels will overlap the side panels by 5/8" on each side).

Cut the ten cleats long enough to fit in the positions shown in the diagram on page 21—there should be a little space between the ends of the cleats, so exact cutting is not important. Just make sure the edges are flush with the edges of the panel they are attached to.

Fasten four cleats along the perimeter of each side panel, using 2" deck screws.

Fasten the remaining two cleats at the edges of the back side of the center panel.

Set the center panel between the side panels so the front is aligned with the peak in the roof. Make sure the center panel is perpendicular; then attach it with 2" deck screws driven through the side panels and into the cleats at the edges of the center panel (photo 5).

ATTACH THE ROOF & TRIM

The roof and trim are the final structural elements to be fastened to the doghouse.

Cut the house roof and porch roof to size from ¾"-thick exterior plywood, with a finish-grade face.

Fasten the roof panels to the cleats at the tops of the side walls, making sure the edges of the panels butt together to form the roof peak.

Cut the trim pieces to frame the roof from 1 x 2 cedar. The end roof trim pieces are square-cut at the ends, but the ends of the side roof trim pieces need to be miter-cut to form clean joints at the peak and at the ends, where they meet the end trim. To mark the side trim pieces for cutting, first cut the side trim pieces so they are an inch or two longer than the space between the end of the roof panel and the roof peak. Lay each rough trim piece in position, flush with the top of the roof panel. On each trim piece, mark a vertical cutoff line that is aligned with the end of the roof panel. Then, mark a cutoff line at the peak, making sure the line is perpendicular to the peak. Cut the trim pieces with a power miter saw or miter box and backsaw.

Attach the trim pieces to the side panels with 6d galvanized finish nails (photo 6).

APPLY FINISHING TOUCHES

Sand all the wood surfaces smooth, paying special attention to any sharp edges, then prime and paint the doghouse. Use a good-quality exterior primer and at least two coats of paint, or you can do as we did and simply apply two or three coats of nontoxic sealant to preserve the natural wood tones. We used linseed oil.

Cut a strip of galvanized steel flashing to cover the roof peak (or you can use aluminum flashing, if you prefer). Use tin snips or aviator snips to cut the flashing, and buff the edges with emery paper to help smooth out any sharp points.

Lay the flashing lengthwise on a wood scrap, so the flashing overhangs by 2". Bend the flashing over the edge of the board to create a nice, crisp peak, then attach the flashing with roofing nails with neoprene (rubber) washers driven at 4" intervals (photo 7).

Scale Your Plans

If plan dimensions do not meet your needs, you can recalculate them to a different scale. The doghouse shown here is designed for an average dog (about 15" tall). If you own a larger dog, add 1" to the size of the entry cutouts and panels for every inch that your dog is taller than 15".

Install metal flashing over the roof peak, using roofing nails with rubber washers.

Insulated Doghouse

Flat-roof doghouses are found throughout the world. Often constructed with a slight slope to the roof, these doghouses are easy to insulate with insulation board, and if they are sized appropriately they keep dogs warmer than a house with a peaked roof. In warm weather, the roof can be propped open slightly for ventilation. The inner partition can be omitted in southern climes. In the wintry north, a door cover will help keep the heat in (see "Dog Door" in the Accessories chapter).

This doghouse sports a simple exterior plywood roof that was sealed with three coats of enamel porch paint. If you live in a wet or cold climate, adding a roof covering, such as fully bonded asphalt roll roofing, is a good idea. The interior walls and ceiling of the sleeping area are insulated and have hardboard wall coverings.

Tools, Materials & Cutting List

- Measuring tape
- Marker
- Square
- Circular saw
- Drill/driver
- Utility knife
- Hammer
- Caulk gun
- Paintbrush
- Brad nailer (optional)
- Deck screws
- Box nails
- Caulk
- Panel adhesive
- Hinges (3)

- Exterior primer and paint
- 1½" galvanized casing nails
- (2) 2 × 4" × 10' pressure treated pine
- (6) 2 × 2" × 8' framing lumber
- ½" sheet of ¾" exterior plywood
- (2) ½" × 4 × 8' exterior plywood
- (1) 1½" × 4 × 8' rigid foam insulation
- (1) ⅛" × 4 × 8' tempered hardboard

Key	Part	Dimension	Pcs.	Material
A	Joists	1½ × 3½ × 29"	4	PT
B	Rim joists	1½ × 3½ × 48"	2	PT
C	Floor	¾ × 48 × 32"	1	¾" Ply
D	Front and back wall	¾ × 30/33 × 48"	2	½" Ply
E	Tall wall	½ × 33 × 33"	1	½" Ply
F	Short wall	½ × 30 × 33"	1	½" Ply
G	Partition wall	½ × 30 × 19"	1	½" Ply
H	Left stud front wall	1½ × 1½ × 27⅞"	1	Pine
I	Top plate front wall	1½ × 1½ × 48"	1	Pine
J	Right stud front wall	1½ × 1½ × 25"	1	Pine
K	Middle stud front wall	1½ × 1½ × 27"	1	Pine
L	Sill plate front wall	1½ × 1½ × 48"	1	Pine
M	Sill and top plate, tall & short walls	1½ × 1½ × 29"	4	Pine
N	Studs for partition	1½ × 1½ × 27"	2	Pine
O	Top plate partition	1½ × 1½ × 29"	1	Pine
P	Bottom plate partition	1½ × 1½ × 19"	1	Pine
Q	Back wall top plate, hinge side	1½ × 3½ × 48"	1	Pine
R	Back wall right stud	1½ × 1½ × 23"	1	Pine
S	Back wall middle stud	1½ × 1½ × 25"	1	Pine
T	Back wall left stud	1½ × 1½ × 26"	1	Pine
U	Roof	½ × 56 × 41"	1	½" Ply
V	Flat-to-roof edge frame	1½ × 3½ × 34"	2	Pine
W	Flat-to-roof edge frame	1½ × 3½ × 56"	2	Pine
X	Roof insulation frame	1½ × 1½ × *	4	Pine
Y	Siding batten	¾ × 1½ × *	16	Pine
Z	Ramp board	1½ × 3½ × 36"	3	Pine
AA	Ramp tread	¾ × 1½ × 9"	4	Pine
BB	Ramp cleat	¾ × 1½ × 10"	1	Pine

* *Cut to fit.*

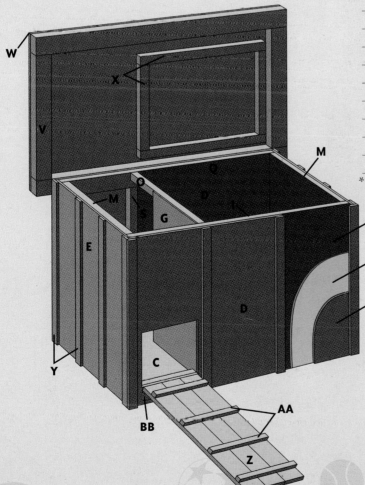

Hardboard

Insulation

Siding

How to Build an Insulated Doghouse

Connect the rim joists and the floor joists with 3" deck screws. For pressure-treated lumber, be sure to use stainless steel, hot-dipped galvanized, or coated screws.

Lay out the trapezoidal shapes for the side walls and cut the panels to size and shape with a circular saw and straightedge cutting guide.

BUILD THE FLOOR AND WALLS

The floor is made of exterior grade ¾" plywood set onto 2 × 4 pressure-treated joists. The joists are offset slightly so the partition wall can be located above a joist when it is installed. Cut the joists and rim joists to size. Lay out the joists between the rim joists with one at each end and the others located 14" in from the ends. Drill pilot holes and drive two 3" screws through the rim joists into each joist end (photo 1).

Cut the floor and wall panels to size using a circular saw and straightedge (photo 2). Note that the front and back walls slope downwards from 33" high to 30" high to create a slight roof pitch for rain and snow runoff. Cut the panels so that when the house is assembled, the better grade face on the plywood will be facing out. Mark the angled top cuts for the wall studs by holding them against the angled edge of the panel.

On the back face of the front wall panel, outline the door 3" from the left edge of the wall (when viewed from the outside of the doghouse) and 3½" up from the bottom. Size the opening according to your dog's height (see Minimum/Maximum Sizing, p. 29). Drill a starter hole in the outline. Use a jigsaw to cut the door opening (photo 3).

Cut the framing members to size except for the front and back top plates. Draw lines on the inside faces of the wall panels, 2" up from the bottoms (photo 4). Attach the sills above these lines with 1⅝" screws from the outside. Use this method to attach all framing to the walls. On the side-wall sills, leave a 2" gap between the sill ends and the sides of the panels. Attach the side-wall top plates to the top insides of the walls, also leaving a 2" gap at the plate ends.

This house fits a medium-size dog like a Springer Spaniel or Border Collie. Adjust the dimensions of your doghouse to the size of your dog. At minimum:

- The bottom-to-top height of the door opening must equal the depth (D) of your dog plus 1".
- The length and width of the sleeping area must approximately equal the length (L) of the dog from nose to rump (tail excluded).
- The height of the ceiling should exceed the dog's standing height (H) by 25%.

If the dog will use the house to stay warm, do not exceed minimum sizing by more than 25%.

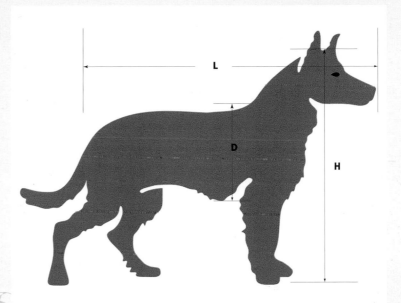

Dogs need less room than you might expect, and benefit in cold weather from a close-fitting house.

Cut out the door opening with a jigsaw. You can either make a plunge cut with the saw or drill a starter hole for the saw blade.

Lay out locations for the individual wall framing members on the inside surfaces of the wall panels.

Attach each individual wall panel to the wall framing members with deck screws driven through the sheathing and into the wall panels.

Attach the studs to the front and back wall panels (photo 5). Align the left and right studs with the ends of the panel. Align the middle studs between lines 33" and 34½" from the high side of the panels. Note that the back studs are shorter than the front studs to accommodate the 2 × 4 top plate. Cut the front and back top plates to fit and attach. You may trace the angle lines directly on the plates by positioning them in the walls.

ATTACH THE WALLS

Attach the wall sections to the deck with 2½" screws driven every 8" through the sill plates. Attach the side walls to the front and back walls by driving 2" screws through the plywood into the framing. Attach the partition wall to the partition wall framing. Align the partition wall ¾" offset from the middle stud, so the hardboard interior

can be attached to the studs later (photo 6). Attach the partition wall to the floor (photo 7).

BUILD & INSTALL THE ROOF

Cut the plywood roof panel to size and the 2 × 4 roof frame members to length. The roof framing is aligned with the perimeter of the roof and is attached with the 2 × 4 faces against the underside of the roof. Attach the framing to the roof. Cut the roof insulation frames to size so the square frame fits inside the sleeping area walls when the roof is closed. Test-fit the roof. There should be approximately a ½" gap between the roof framing and the wall sides. Install the roof framing. Screw three utility hinges to the back exterior wall panel, located 1½" down from the top of the wall sheathing (photo 8).

Pre-drill pilot holes into the offset partition and wall studs and attach the wall with 3" screws. The offset provides attachment surfaces on both walls for hardboard insulation covering.

Secure the sill plate for the partition wall to the doghouse floor with deck screws.

Attach three utility hinges, spaced evenly, along the back wall and roof perimeter frame. The barrels of the hinges should be 1½" beneath the top edge of the back wall.

INSULATE & COVER WALLS

Cut 1½"-thick rigid foam insulation board into panels that fit within the stud wall openings inside the sleeping area (photo 9). Use a utility knife to cut the insulation. Also cut insulation board to fit inside the ceiling frame on the underside of the roof panel. Using a non-solvent based panel adhesive, attach the insulation to the walls, roof and underside of the floor. Then, cut wall and ceiling coverings from ⅛"- or ¼"-thick tempered wall panels. Install the wall panels with 1" paneling nails (photo 10).

Cut pieces of 1½"-thick rigid foam insulation board to fit into the stud wall cavities and roof frame. Score the insulation with a utility knife, then snap it.

Cover the insulated walls inside the sleeping area with tempered hardboard panels. Also cover the ceiling insulation and frame with hardboard.

FINISH THE HOUSE

As a decorative touch, cut 1 × 2 battens to fit on the walls and at the corners, extending from the bottom to the top of the wall sheathing. Nail a batten at each corner and add two intermediate battens, evenly spaced, per wall (photo 11).

If your dog is on the small side, build him or her a ramp from 2 × 4 and 1 × 2 scrap, then screw the top end of the ramp to a 1 × 2 cleat mounted beneath the door opening (photo 12). If you have a larger dog, don't install a ramp—it will only be an impediment.

Prime, paint, or stain the house. For the roof, apply at least three coats of exterior enamel porch paint. Ideally, you should position the doghouse in a sheltered spot in your yard.

Cut strips of 1 × 2 pine to create battens that fit between the bottoms and tops of the exterior sheathing. Install four battens per side, spaced evenly and at each corner.

Paint the doghouse and the battens with exterior paint. If you own a smaller dog, build a simple ramp from 2 × 4 and 1 × 2 scraps, paint it to match, and attach it to a cleat beneath the door opening.

Green Doghouse

This "green" doghouse, with its sod roof and stucco siding, stays cooler in the summer and warmer in the winter. A sod roof, like the one featured, may become a favorite lookout perch for your pooch. Though this house is stucco, it could be sided to match your own house.

Tools, Materials & Cutting List

- Measuring tape
- Marker
- Square
- Circular saw
- Hand saw
- Drill/driver
- Utility knife
- Hammer
- Caulk gun
- Stapler
- Paintbrush
- Jig saw
- Clamps
- Straightedge
- Trowel
- 2" hole saw
- (2) 8' pressure treated 2 × 4s
- (1) 4' pressure treated 4 × 4
- 2 sheets 4 × 8' ¾" CDX plywood
- 1 half sheet (4 × 4') ¾" p.t. plywood
- (3) 8' 2 × 3s (pine)
- (6) 8' 2 × 2s (pine)
- (1) 6' 1 × 3 (cedar)
- (4) 10' 1 × 4 (cedar)
- 2" deck screws
- 3½" deck screws
- 2" galvanized casing nails
- Staples
- ¾" roofing nails
- 36" long 27/16" drip edge
- Two 2" circular louver vents
- Roll 15 lb. building paper
- ½ sheet ⅝" cement board (optional)
- Planting medium
- Sod
- 12 ft. aluminum drip edge
- 3 × 12 ft. stucco lath
- 10 ft. stucco lath corner
- Fencing staples

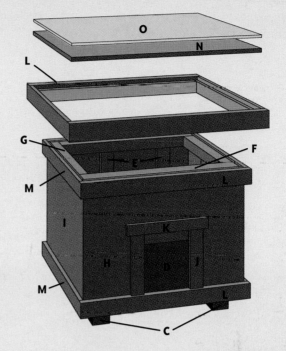

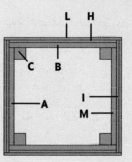

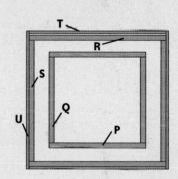

Key	Part	Dimensions	Pcs.	Material
A	Floor joist	1½ × 3½ × 29"	3	PT 2 × 4
B	Joist header	1½ × 3½ × 32"	2	PT 2 × 4
C	Feet	3½ × 3½ × 6"	4	PT 4 × 4
D	Floor deck	¾ × 32 × 32¾"	1	CDX ply.
E	Wall studs	1½ × 2½ × 22½"	9	2 × 3 Pine
F	Front & back top plate	1½ × 1½ × 32"	2	2 × 2 Pine
G	Side top plates	1½ × 1½ × 29"	2	2 × 2 Pine
H	Front/back wall sheathing	¾ × 32 × 27¾"	2	CDX ply.
I	Side wall sheathing	¾ × 33½ × 27¾"	2	CDX ply.
J	Door trim - side	¾ × 2½ × 12¼"	2	Cedar
K	Door trim - top	¾ × 2½ × 16¾"	1	Cedar

Key	Part	Dimensions	Pcs.	Material
L	Front/back frieze/base	¾ × 3½ × 35¼"	4	Cedar
M	Side frieze/base	¾ × 3½ × 33½"	4	Cedar
N	Roof deck	¾ × 39 × 40"	1	CDX ply.
O	Sod underlayment	⅝ × 39 × 40"	1	Cement board
P	Frame stops f/b	1½ × 1½ × 28½"	2	2 × 2 Pine
Q	Frame stops side	1½ × 1½ × 25½"	2	2 × 2 Pine
R	Deck frame f/b	1½ × 1½ × 39"	2	2 × 2 Pine
S	Deck frame side	1½ × 1½ × 36½"	2	2 × 2 Pine
T	Roof fascia f/b	¾ × 3½ × 40½"	2	Cedar
U	Roof fascia side	¾ × 3½ × 40½"	2	Cedar

How to Build a Green Doghouse

1

Drive deck screws through the second header and into the end of the outside joist, completing the 2 × 4 frame for the floor.

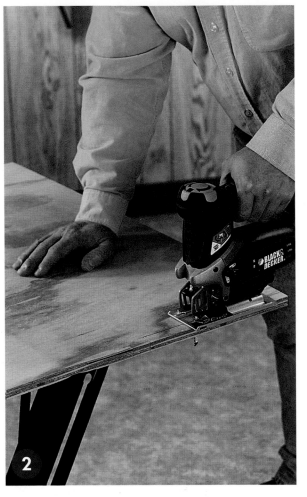

2

Finish the threshold tongue cutout, using a jig saw.

BUILD THE FLOOR AND STUD WALLS

Cut the floor joists and headers to length from pressure-treated 2 × 4 lumber. Drive a pair of 3½" deck screws through pilot holes in the ends of each header and into the outside joists to make a square frame (photo 1). Use a carpenter's square to check for square. Press the corner into square if necessary, and then add the center joist between the headers.

Cut the floor deck to size from exterior grade (CDX) plywood. Start by cutting your plywood stock so it is 32 × 33½" in size. Then, draw a reference line ¾" back from and parallel to one long end. Measure in 11" from each end of the reference line and draw a cutting line that extends from the edge of

the plywood to the reference line. Cut out the ¾" by 11" waste section from each end, creating a ¾" × 10" tongue that will serve as the threshold of the doghouse (photo 2).

Cut the wall studs to length. If your local lumberyard does not stock 2 × 3s, use full-width 2 × 4s, or rip-cut a 2 × 6 down the middle to create pairs of 2 × 3s (approximately). Position the studs on the top surface of the deck and trace around them for reference. Then, flip the deck on its edge and drive two or three 3½" deck screws up through the underside of the deck and into the bottom end of each stud (photo 3). After all of the wall studs are attached to the deck floor, position the deck over the floor frame so all of the outside edges align. Drive 2" deck screws down through the plywood deck and into the tops of the floor frame members. Drive screws every 8" (photo 4).

Cut the top plates for the front, back, and side to length and then attach them to the tops of the wall studs with 3½" deck screws (photo 5). Drill pilot holes first so you don't split the 2 × 2 plates. Test the stud walls with a framing square and adjust as necessary.

Flip the structure so the top plates are resting on a flat surface, then cut the feet to length. Attach the feet by driving a pair of 3½" screws through each 2 × 4 in the frame corner. The tops of the feet should be resting on the underside of the floor deck. It isn't necessary to drive screws down through the deck.

INSTALL THE SHEATHING AND TRIM
Cut the wall sheathing from ¾" CDX plywood. Use a circular saw and straightedge cutting guide or a table saw to make square cuts (photo 6).

Outline the door opening in the front wall sheathing piece (see drawing, p. 23). Drill a starter hole in one corner of the cutout and then make the cutout with a jig saw, squaring off the corners as you go (photo 7). If the cutout is uneven, smooth it with a belt sander or random orbit sander.

3

Drive a 3½" deck screw through the bottom of the floor deck and into a wall stud. Have a helper hold the stud, if possible.

4

Attach the deck (with the studs attached to the deck but loose on top) to the floor frame with deck screws.

Drive a deck screw down into the last top plate to complete the stud walls.

Cut out the wall sheathing panels from CDX plywood, using a circular saw and straightedge guide.

Drill starter holes and then make the door cutout in the front wall sheathing.

Attach the front piece of wall sheathing to the framing last.

Staple one long piece of building paper all around the doghouse, then trim the top. Cut out the door opening with a utility knife (cut from the inside, following the door opening edges).

Use galvanized finish nails to nail the front base trim piece in place.

Attach wall sheathing to the wall and floor framing with 1⅝" deck screws. Apply the front and back panels first. The threshold tongue should fit through the door opening (photo 8).

Staple 15-pound building paper (use two layers for stucco) to the doghouse walls. Wrap the entire house with one course of building paper so the bottom edge of the paper is flush with the bottom edge of the sheathing. Staple the building paper every eight square inches or so, then trim off the excess at the top and cut out the door opening (photo 9).

Cut the base trim boards to size. Using 2" galvanized finish nails, attach the front trim piece so the top edge is flush

with the top of the floor deck. The ends should overhang the sheathing by ¾" on each side (photo 10).

Attach the side and back trim boards with finish nails, making sure the top edges of the trim boards are level with the top of the front base trim board.

Attach the top trim/frieze boards so the top edges are all even with the top edges of the sheathing and the stud wall caps. If the sheathing panels are not quite level with one another, install the trim so the tops are level with the lowest point on the wall sheathing and each board is parallel with the base trim beneath it.

11

Attach the head casing so the overhang on the side casing is equal.

12

Nail aluminum drip-edge flashing so it fits over the top edges of the base trim pieces.

Attach the two door casing trim pieces so they rest flush on the top edge of the base trim and are flush with the edges of the door opening. Cap the side trim pieces with the cap trim, centering the cap piece so the overhang is equal on both edges (it should be 1" per side) (photo 11).

Mount a 2"-dia. hole saw in your power drill and drill two 2" holes into the back wall, centered side to side and about 2" down from the top. Insert 2" dia. circular louvers into the hole so the flange is about ⅜" away from the wall on the outside of the doghouse. You'll need to work around the louvers as you install the stucco, but it is easier than trying to cut through the stucco after it is applied.

APPLY THE STUCCO FINISH

Using ½" roofing nails, nail drip-edge flashing to the doghouse walls so the drip-edge covers and overhangs slightly the base trim. Make a relief cut and miter the corners of the flashing. The drip edge will direct moisture away from the trim pieces (photo 12). Drill 2"-dia. vent holes near the top of the back panel and insert round, louvered vent covers (photo 13).

Attach stucco lath (self-furring expanded metal lath) to the walls of the doghouse using galvanized fencing staples (photo 14). At the corners, attach stucco edging using 1½" roofing nails. Also attach edging (or drip screed) at the bottom edges of the walls. Cut the lath with aviator snips so it fits around the circular louvers on the back wall.

A traditional three-coat stucco finish is always best, but if you wish to take a shortcut here, trowel preformulated stucco mix over the lath, following the manufacturer's directions on the container (photo 15). You can find this product at most home building centers or at your local concrete supplies dealer. Paint the stucco, if desired, after it has dried.

> **Tip**
>
> To keep your grass roof groomed, don't use your lawnmower. Use a string trimmer, or give your rabbit a break from his hutch (page 38) and let him munch on the grass a few times each week.

13

Drill two 2"-dia. holes in the back panel, near the top to create openings for round louver vent covers.

14

Attach stucco edging to the corners of the doghouse, using 1½" roofing nails. Stucco lath should already be attached.

15

Apply premixed stucco (or a traditional stucco finish if you prefer) over the stucco lath according to the manufacturer's directions.

BUILD THE GRASS ROOF

The grass roof on this doghouse, while optional, is responsible for much of the structure's charm and efficiency. There is no standard way to construct a grass doghouse roof, but the main points are to make it leakproof, strong enough to support the sod, and to create some allowance for drainage.

Cut the plywood roof deck to size and coat it with waterproof deck sealer. Cut a piece of ⅝"-thick cement board to the same size. Cut cement board the same way you cut wallboard: score it with a utility knife and straightedge and then snap it over a 2 × 4 (photo 16).

The cement board is an optional underlayment for the sod. It is not waterproof, but it will not disintegrate and prevents the sod from skidding or sliding. You can use two or three layers of 6-mil plastic instead.

Cut the deck frame pieces to length and attach them around the underside of the deck frame by driving 1⅝" deck screws down through the plywood and into the frame pieces. Also cut and install the stop frame that will fit inside the roof opening, centering the frame so it will be inset 3½" from all edges of the plywood deck. To create controlled roof runoff, cut a piece of 2⁷⁄₁₆" drip-edge flashing the same length as the width of the roof deck (in

Cut a subbase for the sod roof from cementboard or a waterproof membrane.

Drive galvanized finish nails through the back fascia and into the front ends of the side fascia pieces.

Cover the roof with sod. Unless you have a ready supply of replacement sod, lay down a layer (1" or so) of growing medium.

the back). Nail the drip edge to the top, back edge of the plywood deck. Then, apply construction adhesive to the underside (the smooth side) of the cementboard and place it on top of the plywood, capturing the edge of the drip edge between the layers. Caulk around the edges.

Cut the fascia to length. Attach the front fascia board with construction adhesive and 2" finish nails (galvanized) driven into the roof frame. The bottom edge of the fascia should be flush with the bottom edge of roof frame, leaving about ½" projecting above the surface of the roof deck. Attach the side fascia so the tops are flush with the front fascia, and then drive two nails through each

end of the front fascia to lock-nail the side fascia pieces to it. Then attach the back fascia piece by driving finish nails through its face and into the ends of the side fascia boards. This should create a ½" drainage gap between the back fascia and the roof deck (photo 17).

Position the doghouse in your yard. To improve drainage, shim under the front legs about ¼" to pitch the doghouse toward the drainage gap in the back edge of the roof. Set the roof onto the house. Cut sod to fit and cover roof with it (photo 18). Water sod frequently, as it will be vulnerable to drying out (positioning the house in partial shade will help prolong the life of the sod).

Dog Beds

Mᴏꜱᴛ ᴏꜰ ᴜꜱ ᴡᴀɴᴛ ᴏᴜʀ ᴄᴀɴɪɴᴇ ᴄᴏᴍᴘᴀɴɪᴏɴꜱ ᴛᴏ ꜱʟᴇᴇᴘ ɪɴ ᴄᴏᴍꜰᴏʀᴛ. ᴀɴᴅ ᴀꜱ ᴡɪᴛʜ ᴇᴠᴇʀʏᴛʜɪɴɢ ᴇʟꜱᴇ ᴅᴏɢ, ʙᴇᴅꜱ ᴄᴏᴍᴇ ɪɴ ᴀ ᴠᴀʀɪᴇᴛʏ ᴏꜰ styles to suit nearly every dog's sleeping preferences. Does your dog prefer sleeping stretched out? Then a rectangular or oval bed is best. Does your dog like to sleep curled up in a ball? Then choose a round bed. Does your dog like to lean against something while he sleeps? Then a bolster or nesting bed is your best bet.

The options don't stop with shape. You can find elevated cot-like beds, orthopedic beds, heated beds, and plain old mats. The materials these beds are made of vary too. Cotton, jute, microfiber, and canvas are just some of the choices. Even the stuffing varies. Cedar shavings add a pest repellent feature to a dog bed, but you can also find beds stuffed with polyfil, foam, and poly/cotton. For a truly personalized look, you can order or make your own custom dog bed. Online manufacturers of bench cushions will create a dog bed made of your choice of fabric, padding, and decorative features. Most important, though, is a removable cover for easy washing—unless the whole bed can be thrown into the washer.

The Comfort of Denning

The dog's roots go way back in history to a wilder time before civilization. Wolves, the ancestors of dogs, found safety and shelter in dens—natural cavities in the earth. Dens are so safe that mother canids trust them as sanctuaries to birth their pups.

Modern dogs have the same instinct to seek shelter that their ancestors had. Today, though, dogs have to make do under tables or chairs or anywhere else in the house that can give them a sense of physical protection. Consider placing your dog's bed in a den-like, protected area of the house. If you provide a "den" for your dog in the form of a crate, don't be surprised if he eagerly settles into it right away.

A Place of One's Own

Most dogs know just what to do when they see their first bed. Some, though, may need a bit of coaxing. If you have such a dog, try luring him to the bed with a treat or toy. It's a good idea to use a word your dog will always associate with the bed so you can direct him there whenever you need him in one spot. Follow this protocol even if your dog's bed is in a crate.

A dog's bed can be placed anywhere in the house that is dry and free of drafts. Some dogs like to be a part of the action, in which case you may want to place your dog's bed in the kitchen or rec room. Other dogs prefer calm and quiet. A bedroom may be a better location for these peace-seeking pooches.

You can go a step further and create a "den" for your dog that can be used as a piece of furniture in your home—a nightstand or end table, for instance.

Although many people enjoy having their dogs sleep with them, giving your dog his own bed, a place to call his very own, will be comforting to him. That doesn't mean you can't get down and cuddle with your pup—that's always allowed!

Contemporary Dog Bed

So you have more of the angular, no-froufrou kind of style. Well, this dog bed is for you. With its clean lines, chrome legs, and stylish material, this bed would fit into any contemporary or midcentury-style house. The platfrom is made from Baltic Birch plywood and should be sized to match the dimensions of your dog bed mattress.

Tools, Materials & Cutting List

- Measuring tape
- Circular saw
- Straightedge
- Clamps
- Utility knife
- Router with ⅜" piloted roundover bit
- Drill
- Square
- (1) dog bed mat or bench cushion (size as desired)
- Wood finishing materials
- 1 sheet 5 × 5-ft. (or 2 × 4-ft. if available) ¾" Baltic birch plywood
- Wood finishing tools
- (4) 4 to 6" tall legs
- Fine sandpaper
- Round neck pillow
- Hook and loop fastener strips

Key	Part	Dimension	Pcs.	Material
A	Platform top	¾ × 22 × 35"	1	Plywood

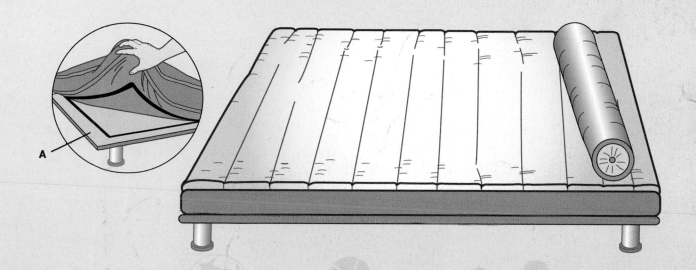

A

How to Build a Contemporary Dog Bed

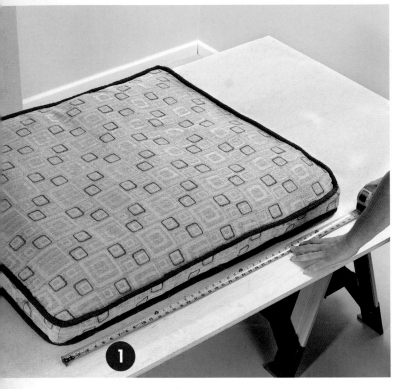

1

Measure the width and length of dog bed mat or bench cushion.

CHOOSE THE MAT

You can build your dog bed to any size or shape you like. It's best to have the bed mat or cushion on hand before building the platform because the plywood top of the platform should match the dimensions of the mat for a neat custom look.

The dog bed shown in this project is designed with a 22"-wide x 35"-long prefabricated mat.

Once you have the mat, carefully measure its outer dimensions to determine the sizing of the platform top (photo 1).

CUT THE PLATFORM TOP

The edges of the plywood top will be exposed in the finished piece, so it's important to make the cuts as straight and clean as possible and to minimize any burn marks from the saw blade. If you're making the cuts with a circular saw, use a straightedge guide to help keep the blade straight, and make sure to keep the saw moving all the way through each cut to prevent burn marks. If possible, use the factory edges for two sides of the top so you have to make only two cuts.

Make the end cut on plywood top with a circular saw and straightedge clamped to top. Make sure the cut is set up at the corner of the sheet to utilize factory edges.

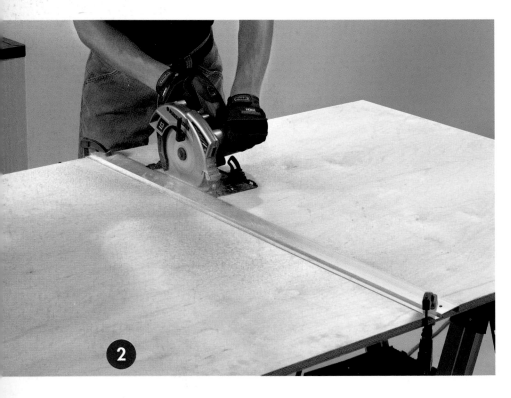

2

Baltic Birch

Baltic birch plywood is a furniture- or cabinet-grade plywood made with thin plies of hardwood and face veneers of blond birch. The plies are virtually free of voids, so exposed edges of Baltic birch look better than those of standard plywood. Baltic birch also has more plies: up to 15, compared to standard plywood's 5 to 9. Baltic birch commonly comes in 5 x 5-ft. sheets and is well priced when compared with the low-grade birch-veneer plywood at home warehouse stores. You can buy Baltic birch through lumberyards and hardwood suppliers.

Mark the cutting lines onto the back side of the plywood (what will be the bottom face) to match the dimensions of your mat. Clamp a straightedge to the workpiece so the saw's blade will be aligned with the cutting line. Note: When cutting across the grain of the face veneers, it's a good idea to make a score cut along the cutting line with a sharp utility knife and a straightedge. This helps reduce tearout from the saw blade coming up through the wood.

Make the first cut, then reset the straightedge and make the second cut (photo 2).

ROUND OVER THE TOP EDGES

Shaping the edges of the plywood top creates a finished look and eliminates sharp edges and corner points, as well as the potential for splintering. The best way to round over plywood edges is with a router and piloted roundover bit. If you don't have access to a router, you can simply sand the edges with sandpaper and a sanding block to create a slight roundover and eliminate splinters. Just be careful not to sand the face veneers too much; these outer layers are thin and can easily be sanded through.

Set up the router with a ⅜" piloted roundover bit using a scrap piece of plywood to set the desired bit depth (amount of roundover). Make a test cut on a scrap after each adjustment of the bit depth to see precisely how the bit will cut on your workpiece.

Rout along all edges of the platform top with the router base riding along the face of the panel (photo 3). Flip the panel over and repeat to complete the roundover.

Route a roundover on the plywood edge using a ⅜" piloted roundover bit and fixed-base or plunge router. If you don't have a router, sand the edges and corners until they're smooth and rounded.

FINISH THE PLATFORM TOP

Using Baltic birch plywood (or a similar furniture-grade hardwood plywood) means you can leave the edges exposed and finish the top with a stain and/or clear protective top coat, such as polyurethane. The layered edges of the plywood create a subtle decorative effect that works well with simple modern furniture.

Lightly sand all surfaces of the top with fine sandpaper. Be careful when sanding the edges: the alternating layers of end grain and side grain sand away at different rates, and oversanding results in an uneven surface. Also be careful not to sand through the thin face layers.

Stain the top, if desired, or you can retain the wood's natural coloring by applying a clear top coat (all finishes change the color of wood somewhat, so test the finish on scrap material). For the protective top coat, standard brush-on polyurethane does a better job of sealing and smoothing the edges of plywood than penetrating finishes (such as linseed oil or tung oil) or wipe-on polyurethane. Apply all finishes according to the manufacturer's directions (photo 4).

Apply standard (not wipe-on) clear polyurethane to the top face of the platform top. Use a foam brush for water-based urethane, or a natural-bristle brush for oil-based urethane. The top can be stained or not, depending on the color(s) of the mat used.

Mark pilot holes through predrilled holes in the table leg mounting plate. Be sure to use a square to keep the holes even.

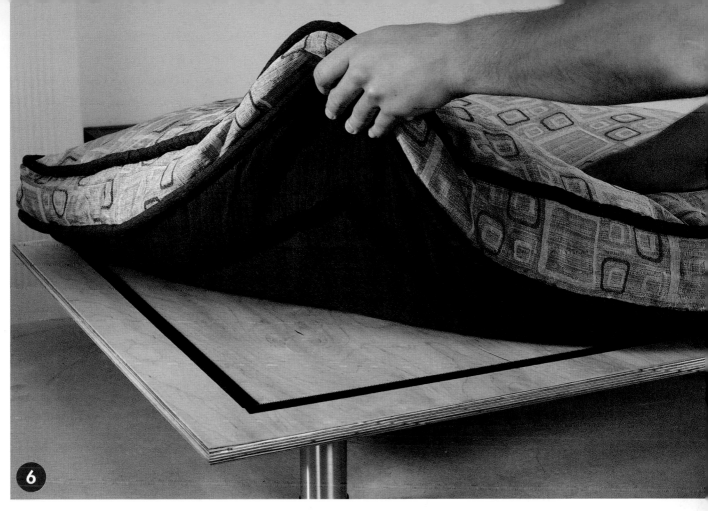

After attaching the Velcro strips to the underside of the bedding, carefully place it on the platform. Place the strips about 2" in from side edges of mat and platform.

INSTALL THE PLATFORM LEGS

The platform legs used here are $^{15}/_{16}$"-diameter x 4"-long round metal table legs with integrated mounting plates that you fasten to the bottom of the platform with screws. Similar legs are available in longer lengths and larger diameters, as well as in square shapes and several finish options. Cutting metal table legs typically is not recommended, so if you want shorter legs, you can buy wood table legs and cut them to the desired size. Wood legs typically have a dowel screw at their top ends that screws into a metal mounting plate fastened to the table surface.

Mark the positions of the table legs onto the bottom face of the platform top, as desired. In the project shown, the legs are centered at 5¾" from the ends and 2" from the side edges of the top.

Position each leg in place, and mark and drill pilot holes for the mounting screws (photo 5). Install the leg with the provided screws (make sure the screws won't go through the top face of the platform).

ADD THE MAT

Depending on your dog's sleeping habits and the type of mat or cushion you choose, you can simply lay down the bedding materials onto the platform to complete the project, or you can secure the mat and/or pillow with hook-and-loop tape (as in photo).

Hook-and-loop tape comes in rolls of self-adhesive strips. A couple of long strips along the sides of the mat are plenty to keep the mat in place. Stick one side (rough side or soft side) of the strips onto the platform in a straight line, parallel to the side edges.

Apply a mating strip over each stuck strip, then peel off the plastic backing on the top strips. Place the mat onto the strips in the desired position, and press down so the strips stick to the bottom side of the mat. Carefully pull up the mat while separating the mating strips (photo 6). Secure the strips to the mat by stitching along the edges, as needed, with a needle and thread.

Nightstand/Bed

If you have a smaller dog, this nightstand/bed is a fun way to incorporate your dog's bed into a prized piece of household furniture. This is a cozy, inviting bed that most dogs will be drawn to because of their denning instinct, yet it's open enough so that your dog will still feel as though he's part of the action.

Tools, Materials & Cutting List

- Tape measure
- Circular saw
- Straightedge
- Clamps
- Utility knife
- Drill
- ⅜" brad point bit
- Jigsaw with fine-tooth plywood blade
- Router with ⅜" piloted roundover bit (optional)
- Bar clamps (4)
- Hammer
- Nail set
- Miter box and backsaw
- Paintbrush or foam roller

- 1 × 2 scrap
- (1) 5 × 5-ft. ¾" Baltic birch plywood
- Square or round dog bed mat or pillow
- Wood glue
- 6d finish nails
- Masking tape
- Medium- and fine-grit sandpaper
- (1) ⅜"-dia. × 36"-long birch (or other hardwood) dowel
- Wood putty
- Wood finish
- (4) 4" metal table legs with mounting screws

Key	Part	Dimension	Pcs.	Material
A	Side box panels	¾ × 18 × 23½"	2	plywood
B	Top/Bottom box panels	¾ × 23½ × 23½"	1 ea.	plywood
C	Back box panel	¾ × 18 × 22"	1	plywood
D	Dowels	⅜"-dia. × 1¾"	18	birch dowel

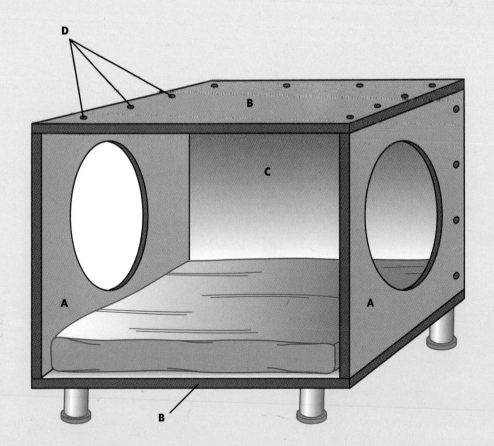

How to Build a Nightstand/Bed

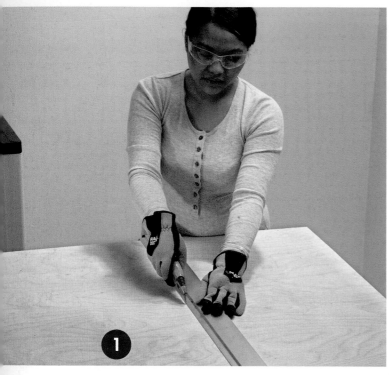

Score along the cutting line with a utility knife using your straightedge as a guide.

Mark a circular cutting line on the center of the side box panel using a 1 × 2 compass.

CUT THE BOX PANELS

This project can be built to any size, so the first step is determining the dimensions of the finished box. If you're using the dog bed as an end table, you'll want the top surface to be at an appropriate height in relation to your other furniture and at a good height for your bed.

The inside dimensions of the box must fit your dog properly, so you may have to alter the proportions of the box to achieve the desired height and interior space. It's a good idea to purchase the bed mat or pillow before finalizing your plans because the right fit and style of the mat makes all the difference in the overall look of the piece.

As shown, the overall dimensions of the dog bed form a 23½" cube, including the 4"-tall legs. Be sure to account for the height of the legs you will use when calculating the box dimensions.

Cut the box panels from a full 5 × 5-ft. sheet of ¾" Baltic birch plywood or a 4 × 8-ft. sheet of other hardwood-veneer plywood. If you plan to paint the box, you can use ¾" MDF instead of plywood. Make the cuts with a circular saw and use a straightedge guide to ensure straight cuts. To prevent burn marks, keep the saw steady and move it continuously through each cut.

MARK THE SIDE CUTOUTS

Each side panel gets a porthole-style cutout in the center of the panel. As shown, the hole is 13" in diameter; the top and bottom edges of the hole are 2½" from the top axnd bottom edges of the panel. If your dog bed is a custom size, subtract from the height of the side panel to find the hole diameter.

Cutting Plywood

Always cut from the least visible side of the plywood (the side that will be concealed most in the finished product). When cutting across the grain of the face veneers, make a score cut along the cutting line with a utility knife to prevent splintering during the saw cut (photo 1).

Mark the center of each side panel by placing a straightedge diagonally along opposing corners of the panel, then tracing along the straightedge near the panel's center. Repeat the process with the straightedge aligned with the other opposing corners to create an X in the panel's center. The intersection of the X is the centerpoint.

Cut a scrap 1 × 2 or a strip of cardboard to about 8" in length. On one end of the stick, use a utility knife to make a small V-shaped notch in the center of the bottom edge. Measure from the notched end and make a mark 6½" (or half the cutout diameter) on the top of the stick. Drill a pilot hole through this mark for a finish nail.

Drive the nail through the pilot hole in the stick and into the centerpoint on the side panel. Set a pencil in the notch of the stick, then rotate the stick in a full circle to create a continuous cutting line with the pencil (photo 2).

COMPLETE THE SIDE CUTOUTS

Drill a starter hole for a jigsaw blade on the interior side of the marked cutout on each side panel using a ¼" or ⅜" drill bit, as appropriate. The outer edge of the starter hole should just touch the cutting line. Complete the cutout with a jigsaw and fine-tooth blade designed for clean plywood cuts (photo 3).

If desired, round over the edges of the cutout using a router and ⅜" piloted roundover bit. When setting the bit depth, be sure to make test cuts on scraps of plywood, and rout the edges on both sides of the scrap so you'll know exactly what the finished edge will look like.

ASSEMBLE THE SIDE AND BOTTOM PANELS

Wipe off all dust from the bottom edges of the side panels and from the top face of the bottom panel. Apply wood glue to the bottom edge of each side panel and set the side panel on top of the bottom panel so all outer edges are flush. Clamp each side panel in place with two bar clamps.

Drill pilot holes through the bottom face of the bottom panel and into the edge of the side panel, and fasten the panels with 6d finish nails. Drive the nails slightly below the surface of the wood with a nail set (photo 4). Tip: To keep the side and bottom panels square while the glue

Make the side hole cutout with a jigsaw and a fine-tooth blade.

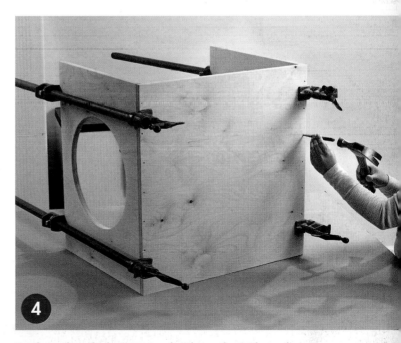

Set the nails in the bottom panel with a nail set. Clamp the side and bottom panels together with two bar clamps on each side.

dries, slip the back panel in between the side panels so it fits tightly against all three panels. Let the glue dry as directed, then remove the clamps.

ADD THE BACK PANEL

Since the outside faces of the side and top panels are exposed, the back and top panels are fastened with hardwood dowels instead of finish nails. This process takes longer than using nails, but the result is a nice hand-built look. If desired, you can use nails in place of dowels following the same process used for the side and bottom panels. Just fill the nail holes on the side and top panels with color-matched wood putty before finishing the piece.

To install the back panel, mark the dowel locations onto the outside face of each side panel ⅜" from the back edge of the panel; locate one dowel ¾" from the top and bottom edges of the side panel and two dowels spaced evenly in between.

Clamp the back brad point panel between the side panels so all outside edges are flush. Apply a band of masking tape around a ⅜" brad point drill bit 1⅞" from the cutting end, or install a depth stop collar at the same location.

Drill a dowel hole at each mark, stopping at the tape on the bit so the hole is 1⅞" deep. Hold the drill level and square to the side panel as you work. Use a sharp bit, and start it slowly to prevent splintering the plywood face veneers.

Cut the dowels to length at 1¾" using a hand miter box and backsaw or a power miter saw.

Remove the back panel, then apply wood glue to its edges and set it back into place. Working on one side at a time, squirt a small amount of glue in each dowel hole, before inserting the dowel into its hole.

Tap the dowels into the holes so they are nearly flush with the plywood surface (photo 5). Wipe up any excess glue with a damp cloth. Quickly complete the same process to secure the other side panel, then clamp the assembly with bar clamps. Let the glue dry.

INSTALL THE TOP PANEL

Prepare and secure the top panel to the side and back panels using the same techniques used when installing the back panel. Locate the dowels ¾" from the front, back, and side edges of the top panel, and space two dowels evenly in between along each edge. Let the glue dry completely.

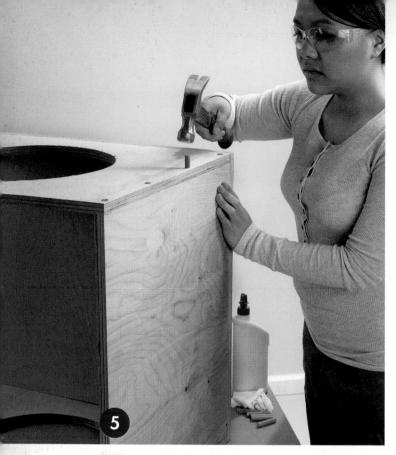

Tap the dowel into the side panel (and edge of back panel) using a hammer or wood mallet. Apply glue sparingly so there's not too much squeeze-out.

Trim ⅜" dowel flush with top panel using backsaw or Japanese saw.

7

Sand a 45° bevel on the front side or front top edge of the completed box using sandpaper and a wood sanding block (not a sanding sponge).

8

Drive a mounting screw through the leg mounting plate and into the bottom panel of the finished box.

Sand the dowels flush to the surrounding surface with medium- and fine-grit sandpapers using a sanding block to prevent unevenness. Be careful not to sand through the thin face veneers of the plywood.

FINISH THE BOX

Sand all surfaces inside and outside the box with fine sandpaper. Also sand or rout a slight bevel or roundover on all of the exposed edges and corners (photo 7).

What to Do about Long Dowels

If any of the dowels is too long to sand, trim it flush (or nearly flush) using a backsaw or Japanese flush-cutting (peg-cutting) saw (photo 6). Be careful not to scratch the plywood face with the saw teeth. Then sand the dowel flush with a random orbit sander.

Fill any chips and nail holes with color-matched wood putty. Let the putty dry, then sand it smooth with fine sandpaper.

Clean the surfaces thoroughly to remove all dust. Apply the stain and/or protective finish of your choice following the manufacturer's directions. Three coats of clear (or with stain added) oil-based polyurethane provides a tough, washable surface that's durable enough for both a dog bed and a tabletop.

INSTALL THE LEGS

Mark the locations of the table legs onto the bottom of the box. In the project shown, the legs are centered about 2" in from the front/back and sides of the box. Hold each leg in place on its layout marks, and mark pilot holes for the mounting screws. Drill the pilot holes and mount the legs with the provided screws (photo 8).

Add the mat or pillow to complete the project.

Mission-Style Dog Bed

A bed frame protects your dog from floor drafts and your couch from the dog. This furniture-quality oak frame can be made to fit any size dog and requires no special woodworking tools. The size of the bed is based on the size of the cushion. Find a rectangular one that fits your needs on the Internet or at a pet store. Then hit your lumberyard or home center for plywood and red oak boards. The bed shown here is sized to accommodate a 30 × 40" dog bed mattress (Note: 30 × 40" pillow-style dog beds are considerably smaller in actual dimensions). This size will be comfortable for dogs up to medium/large in size (75 pounds or so). Always buy your dog mattress first so you can design the bed as needed to fit your dog.

Tools, Materials & Cutting List

- Measuring tape
- Circular saw
- Miter saw
- Hand saw
- Chisel
- Adjustable square
- Miter box with backsaw
- Mallet
- Glue brush
- Clamps
- Nail punch
- Drill/driver and bits
- Hammer
- (3) 1 x 2" x 8' red oak

- (4) 1 x 4" x 8' red oak
- ½ x 30 x 40" oak plywood
- 1½" finish nails
- Wood glue
- 2½" screws
- 1¼" screws
- ⅜" oak dowel or wood plugs
- Sandpaper
- Wood finish or paint

Key	Description	Dimension	Pcs.	Material
A	Front and back frame	¾ x 3½ x 40"	2	Oak
B	Side frame	¾ x 3½ x 28½"	2	Oak
C	Legs	¾ x 2½ x 4"	4	Oak
D	Front and back ledger	¾ x 1½ x 37"	2	Oak
E	Side ledger	¼ x 1½ x 23½"	2	Oak
F	Cushion platform	¼ x 28¼ x 38¼"	1	Oak ply
G	Baluster	¾ x 2½ x 8"	7	Oak
H	Side rail	¾ x 2½ x 25½"	2	Oak
I	Back rail	¾ x 2½ x 38½"	1	Oak
J	Back rail cap	¾ x 1½ x 41¼"	1	Oak
K	Side rail cap	¾ x 1½ x 28¾"	2	Oak

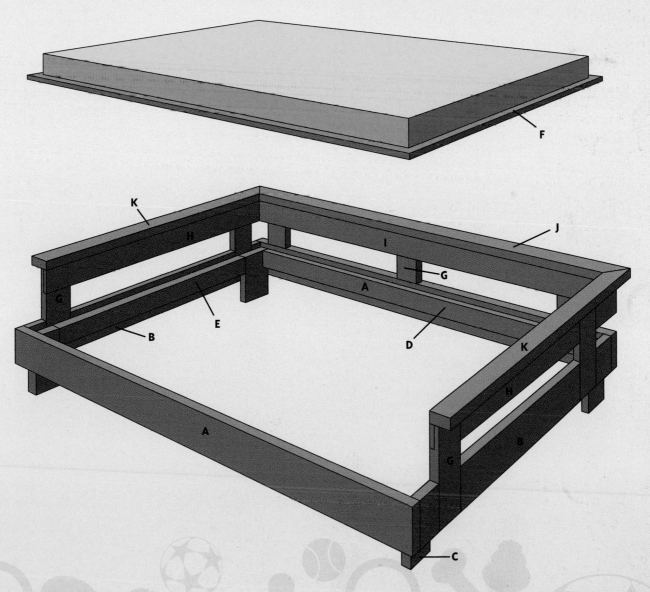

How to Build a Mission-Style Dog Bed

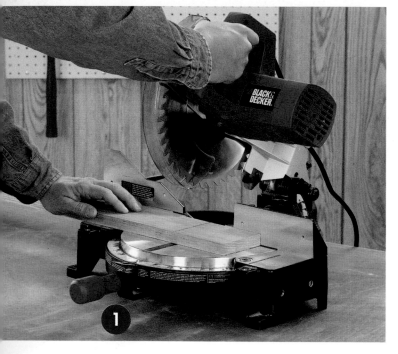

1

Cut the bed parts to length from dimensional oak lumber (or another wood species of your choice).

PREPARE THE PARTS

Measure the cushion or mattress and revise the parts cutting list (page 51) to correspond to the size (existing dimensions are based on a 30" × 40" dog bed). Cut all the parts to length (photo 1).

The frames and rails are attached to the balusters with half-lap joints so the frame and rail surfaces are flush with the baluster surfaces. Each baluster has a 3½" lap cut into one end for the frame, and a 2½" lap cut into the other end for the rail.

Use a table saw mounted dado blade, a router, or a saw and chisel to make the laps. Directions given here are for using a hand saw and chisel. Mark the width and depth of the lap cuts on the balusters, using an adjustable square. Cut along the notch side of each scored line using

2

Make shoulder cuts for the half-lap joints using a back saw and a cutting guide or miter box. Then, make clearance cuts every ¼" to ½" between the shoulder cuts. All cuts should be to ⅜" depth.

a miter box and back saw. The cut is complete when the saw has reached the depth lines on both edges of the board. Cut the edges of the lap cut (called the shoulders) first (photo 2). Then, make a series of depth cuts between the shoulder cuts to make it easier to chisel out the waste. All saw cuts should be to 3/8" depth.

Clear out the wood between saw cuts with a mallet and a sharp wood chisel. Position the chisel bevel-side-down at first so you don't cut too deep, then smooth the wood down to the level of the saw marks (photo 3). The front frame does not have any lap joints. Make marks for the back frame and rail laps at 2½" in from each end and in the center. Cut the laps. The side frames and rails have laps flush with the front edges and 1¼" in from the back edge. Mark and cut the laps.

Chisel out the waste wood between the shoulder cuts with a sharp wood chisel. Orient the bevel downward and don't try to remove too much waste at once.

Basics of Joinery

The strength and professional look of your dog bed will depend on tight, full glue joints, and properly sized screw holes.

Nailing/gluing:
- Paint glue thinly on all mating surfaces of the lap joints and clamp until set.
- Drive nails from legs and ledgers into frames at an angle for strength and so the points stay in the wood. Set the heads of the nails below the surface with a nail punch.
- Scrape and sand off glue squeezed out after the glue is dry. Wiping wet glue can seal the wood and lead to uneven staining.

Driving wood screws:
- Angle top and bottom screws toward the middle of the board for strength.
- Drill a 1/8" hole the full depth of the screw for the threads; drill a 3/16" hole to 1" for the shank, and drill a 3/8" counterbore hole 3/8" deep for the head and dowel.
- Use a #3 driver bit to drive the screw.

ASSEMBLE THE BED FRAME

Glue and clamp the balusters, frames, and rails for each of the three sides.

Cut the legs to length. Outline the exact positions of the legs and ledgers on the bed frames. Glue, clamp, and nail the ledgers and legs to the side frames, and attach the ledgers to the front and back frames. Do not nail into the notches until the balusters are in place (photo 4).

Glue and clamp the balusters to the rails and bed frames (photo 5).

Drill counterbored pilot holes; then screw and glue the front and back frames to the legs and side frames. Taking care to avoid screws already in the joint, drill counterbored pilot holes and screw the side rails to the back rails (photo 6).

Attach the rail caps to the rails, mitering the back corner joints (photo 7). Drill a counterbored pilot hole for each screw. The rail caps overhang the rails to the outside by 3/4".

Attach the ledgers and legs to the inside faces of the side frames with glue and clamps, and then reinforce the joints with countersunk 1¼" wood screws.

Glue and clamp the balusters to the side and back frames, creating the lap joints.

Drill counterbored pilot holes and then glue and screw the side rail and frames to the back rail and frame.

Attach the rail caps to the rails with glue and counterbored screws. Miter the joints where the side rail caps meet the back rail cap.

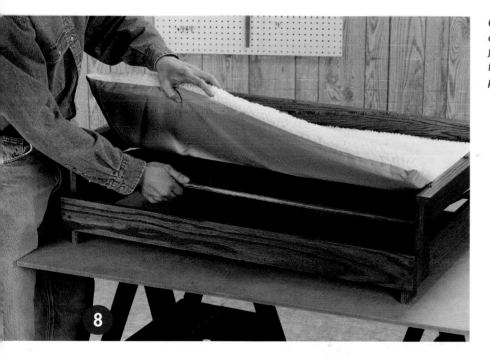

Glue wood plugs into the counterbores and then sand and finish the bed. Rest the platform on the ledgers and lay the mattress or pad on the platform.

FINISH THE BED

Glue dowel plugs into the counterbore holes. When the glue is dry, cut the plugs close with a back saw or flush-cutting saw, and then sand smooth. For a bit of extra design appeal, use domed wood plugs on the visible counterbore holes. Break the rail cap edges by sanding lightly and round the rail cap ends slightly at the front of the bed. Paint or finish according to the instructions on your chosen finish product. Drop the plywood platform and dog mattress or pad into the bed frame (photo 8).

Dog Training

Dog agility has become an increasingly popular sport in recent years. It challenges your dog mentally and is a fun way for her to burn off energy. Although not a primary need like food and water, activity is important to a dog's well-being and health, just as it is for us. The fun and challenge of running a timed obstacle course is exciting for an audience to watch and exhilarating for the participants, both those of the four-legged and of the two-legged varieties. Yes, that's correct; human handlers are right in there, directing their dogs through the obstacles.

Many classes are held throughout the country to help you train your dog in agility. The sport is taken seriously, sanctioned by the American Kennel Club (AKC) with rules and equipment requirements. The obstacles are numerous and costly to buy, but they are manageable projects for the beginning DIYer and inexpensive to build. The AKC even makes it easy for you, posting all equipment requirements right on its web site, www.akc.org.

Don't let the AKC's strict requirements for agility equipment and courses scare you off, though; the backyard just-for-fun families can follow these rules loosely. Have a small space to work with? No problem. You can include as many or as few obstacles as you'd like. Here, we're building three of the many agility obstacles that are used in an official agility trial. If you build all three, feel free to rotate or rearrange the equipment to really keep your dog on her toes!

There is nothing stopping you from having a mini-agility course, or even a full-sized one, in your own backyard—except the lack of a fence. Outdoor activities are best enjoyed in a safe environment. That means your agility course should be securely fenced. Many people avoid fencing in their yards because fences block views and are often unsightly. Invisible fences address both these issues. We will walk you through the installation of an invisible fence. Two things to keep in mind are that your dog will need to be trained in the workings of the fence; and although the fence will keep your dog in, it won't keep other critters out.

A-Frame

Your dog will have a blast running up one side of the A-frame and down the other. Just be sure that she steps on the contact zones, the bright yellow area at the lower end of the obstacle, on her way down.

Tools & Materials

- Hammer
- Power sander
- Circular saw
- Straightedge guide
- Power miter saw
- Paint brush
- Paint roller and tray

- Drill/driver and bits
- (2) ¾" × 4 × 8' plywood
- (6) 2 × 2" x 8'
- (2) 3 × 3" brass butt hinges
- 10 ft. porch swing chain
- (2) chain latches (carabiner)
- (4) 1" eye screws

- Anti-skid paint grit
- Paint
- (8) 1 × 2 × 8' furring strips
- 4d (1") galvanized finish nails
- 2" deck screws

How to Build an A-Frame

PREPARE AND PAINT THE PANELS

Fasten two 2 × 2" × 8 ft. edge supports under each outside edge of each panel, using 2" deck screws

Round-over and smooth the edges of the plywood panels and the 1 × 2 slats using 120-grit sandpaper.

Using hammer and nails, attach the battens to each panel, spacing them about 12" apart at the center. Make sure there is at least 4" between any slat and the top edge of the contact zone.

Paint several coats onto the top half of each panel with your contrasting color, alternating between flat latex paint and anti-skid grit to ensure a nonslip surface. Paint several bright yellow coats onto the bottom 42" of each panel, alternating between flat latex paint and anti-skid grit to ensure a non-slip surface (photo 1). This is the contact zone.

ASSEMBLE THE FRAME

Fasten the two panels together at the peak with two door hinges screwed to the undersides of the panels at their meeting point. The hinges should be installed just inside of the studs (photo 2). An additional slat can be cut to fit and installed between the panel and the hinge to add strength in this area if needed for larger dogs.

Lean the two panels against each other, forming an "A" shape. Adjust the position of the panels until the height of the peak is about 5'.

Install eye screws to each panel stud at the approximate midpoint of its length (4'). The eye can face inward underneath the A frame to prevent a potential hazard. Install a length of chain between the two panels on each side (photo 3). One end of the chain should be permanently fastened. On the other end install a latch for quick joining (we used a carabiner lath). Be sure there are no gaps large enough to catch a dog's paw.

Paint several layers onto the bottom 42" of each panel bright yellow, alternating between flat latex paint and grit.

Fasten the two panels together so they can form an "A" by installing two door hinges underneath the panels on the battens at their meeting point.

Install a length of chain between the two panels on each side. Use the carabiner for the latch at one side.

Hoop Jump

The trick to this dog-training device is getting your dog to jump through the hoop, not run under it. Put your dog on a leash and walk her over to the jump. Position her in front of the hoop, and then go to the other side. Make sure the leash goes through the hoop. Lure your dog through the hoop with a treat or a favorite toy and cheerful commands. It may take a few sessions for your dog to catch on; once she does, repeat the exercise while you're standing beside the hoop jump. You will soon be able to take the leash off your dog and watch her fly through like a pro.

Tools & Materials

- Saw or tubing cutter
- (1) section (8 ft.) 4" dia. flexible plastic drain tile (or, a tire with an inside diameter of approximately 24").
- (2) PVC pipes, 1" dia. x 35" long (horizontal poles)
- (4) PVC pipes, 1" dia. x 18" long (stabilizers)
- (2) PVC pipes, 1" dia. x 45" long (uprights)
- (4) 1" dia. 4-way T fittings
- (2) 1"-dia. 90° elbow fittings
- (3) bungee cords

How to Build a Hoop Jump

BUILD THE STAND

Cut the 1"-dia. PVC tubing into the lengths specified in the materials list on the previous page. Attach an elbow fitting to each end of each upright (photo 1). The PVC parts should fit with enough friction to stay together, but if they are too loose you can use some PVC solvent glue to bind them together. Read and follow the usage instructions and safety precautions on the glue can. Fit a 2"-long tubing piece into one open end of an elbow on each upright and then fit the other end into a 4-way T fitting socket (photo 2). Seat a horizontal pole into the top elbow fittings and another into the 4-way T fitting, connecting the uprights. Then, add an 18" stabilizer tube into the opposite open ends of the 4-way T fittings (photo 3).

MAKE & HANG THE HOOP

If you can't find a suitable tire with an inside diameter of about 24", make your own hoop with 4" dia. flexible drain tile tubing. An 8-ft.long piece will make a circle with a just-under 24" inside diameter when the fitted ends are joined (photo 4). You can make the hoop look more appealing to the dog by wrapping it in a pattern of brightly colored electrical tape. Hang the hoop from the top horizontal bar so the height is matched to your dog's height. Add bungee cords to the sides to secure the hoop in the frame (photo 5).

Attach an elbow fitting to each end of each upright tube.

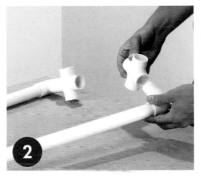

Join the elbow on the base end of each upright to the horizontal connector pole with a 2"-long piece of tubing that's seated in the elbow and in the 4-way T.

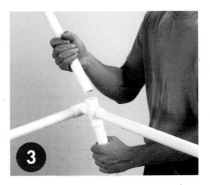

Add stabilizer poles to the base so the frame can stand up.

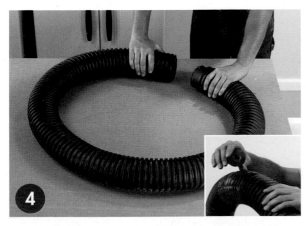

Join the fitted ends on an 8-ft. long piece of 4" drain tile to form a circle. Wrap the hoop with brighty colored electrical tape (inset).

Hang the hoop and secure it to the frame uprights with bungee cords.

Weave Poles

The goal when using weave poles is to have your dog run through the poles slalom-style as quickly as possible without skipping one. If she does miss a pole, take her back to the pole she skipped or any other pole before that one, and get back into the race! Springs and extremely flexible poles can be a danger to dogs, so please don't use them in your construction.

Tools & Materials

- Tubing cutter or saw
- ¾"-dia. PVC tubes: 8 @ 40"; 7 @ 22"; 2 @ 20"; 8 @ 18"; 15 @ 2"
- (16) ¾" T fittings
- (6) ¾" L fittings
- (18) ¾" caps
- Colored tape

How to Build Weave Poles

There are many ways you can cobble together some PVC tubing and fittings to create a network of weave poles. The configuration seen here has the advantage of having only one stabilizer at the intermediate poles. To create it, start by cutting pieces of ¾" PVC tubing to the number and length specified in the materials list on the previous page. You can use a saw, but a tubing cutter makes cleaner cuts and is much safer cutting the 2"-long pieces.

Once you've cut the parts, simply begin to assemble them according to the sequence seen in the photo below. The friction fit should be tight enough to hold all the parts, but if you'll be transporting the weave poles it's a good idea to solvent glue all parts together except the 22"-long connectors. Then you can friction-fit the eight pole assemblies together on-site with the connector poles. Read and follow the safety and usage precautions on the solvent glue can.

For a little color and decoration, create patterns on the poles with colored electrical tape.

The ¾" PVC tubing pieces and the fittings can be assembled with just friction holding the joints together. If you prefer, you can glue some of the key connections for greater stability.

Test-fit all the parts together to make sure they fit right. Disassemble or partially disassemble the project and then reassemble it on site.

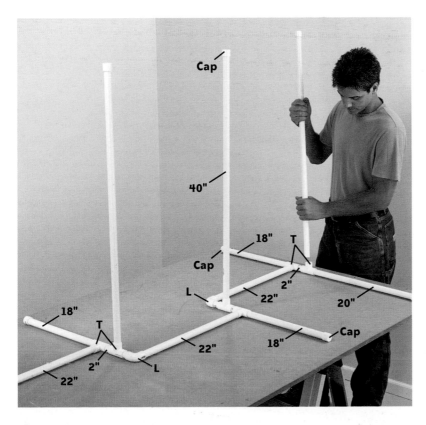

Invisible Fence

An invisible fence consists of a thin electrical wire buried an inch or so underground. It can also be laid into hard walkway and driveway surfaces and can be installed above ground on fences and other fixed structures. This makes it easy to create a continuous barrier to enclose some or all of your property, as well as specific areas inside the boundary such as a garden or swimming pool. Some people even use it to keep boundaries indoors.

The boundary wire receives a constant electrical signal from a small plug-in transmitter located in the garage, house, or other protected space. Your dog wears a collar equipped with a receiver that picks up the signal in the wire and responds accordingly: if your dog approaches the boundary area, the collar beeps and vibrates to warn that the boundary is near. If she continues beyond the warning zone, she is given a mild electrical shock by the collar contacts—a clear message to back away from the boundary. The shock is much like the shock you get from static electricity when you walk along a carpet on a dry day.

Tools & Materials

- Tape measure (100-ft.)
- Drill
- Straightened coat hanger
- Flat spade
- Paint stir stick
- Circular saw and masonry blade
- Concrete or asphalt caulk or patching material
- Shop vacuum
- Eye and ear protection
- Invisible fence kit
- Screws
- Stapler and staples (for wood fence installation only)
- Electrical tape
- Zip ties (for metal fence installation only)
- Wire stripper
- Wire nuts
- Silicone caulk
- Caulk gun
- Work gloves

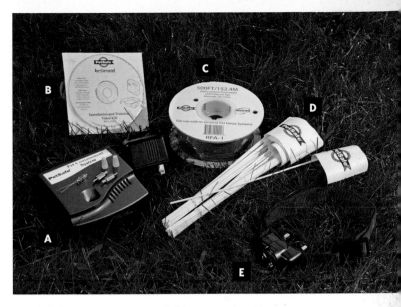

Invisible fence systems are available in complete kits and can be installed in a day. The basic components for installation include (from left to right), a transmitter and power cord (A), installation manual or disc (B), boundary wire (C), boundary flags (D), and a receiver collar (E).

Why an Invisible Fence?

People have many reasons for installing an invisible fence as opposed to a more traditional, visible fence. If the area to be fenced is large, the lower-cost invisible fence may be a more viable option, and some home associations don't allow the "eyesore" of a traditional fence. Invisible fences can also be used inside to keep dogs out of certain areas of the house, as well.

Why Not an Invisible Fence?

There are some potential drawbacks to invisible fences. An invisible fence affects only the dog or dogs whose collars are equipped with a receiver. That means other animals, including other dogs, can cross the boundary into the yard and may pose a threat to the resident dog. Some dogs have a high threshold for pain or will ignore the shock when met with the opportunity to chase a squirrel or neighborhood cat. Sometimes when these dogs come back home, they're unwilling to risk the shock that is bound to occur as they cross back into their yard. And although you may know that your dog isn't going to leave the yard, passersby may get a scare when your dog runs up to the fence to protect her property. As far as strangers can tell, there is no fence.

Training

Once the invisible fence is installed, flags are placed along the fence line. This is the dog's visible cue that a fence is there, but she has to learn this. For the first week, tape down the prongs on the collar so the

Leaving the Yard

When you want to leave the yard with your dog, turn off the system, take off the receiver collar, put the dog on a leash, and then give the heel command and walk out of the yard. This may take some coaxing, so have plenty of treats on hand. Always walk out at the same place, as though you're going through an invisible gate.

dog won't get shocked; she'll just hear the warning beep. With the dog on a leash, walk her toward the fence and as soon as the warning beep is heard, dash in the other direction, tugging at the leash so the dog follows, then praise the dog. After a week or so of this, remove the tape so the prongs are exposed. When the dog responds to the beep or the shock by moving away from the fence, praise her! When the dog responds reliably to the beep/shock, add distractions. Then train off-leash. When the dog is reliable, remove the flags. This process should take about two weeks. Each invisible fence brand comes with its own, more detailed, training instructions. Be sure to read them.

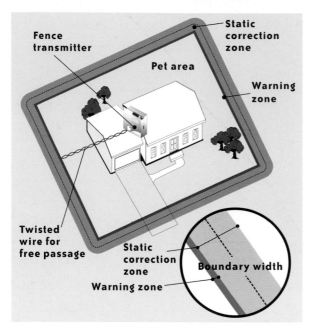

A perimeter layout uses a single run of wire encircling the house and grounds. A single section of twisted wire runs from the boundary to the transmitter. Note: Twisting the boundary wire around itself cancels the signal, creating a "free passage" area for your pet.

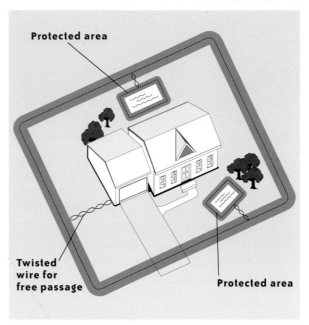

Protecting areas within a perimeter boundary is achieved by looping the wire around the area and returning to the boundary. Twisting the wire between the boundary and protected inner area allows for free passage around the protected area.

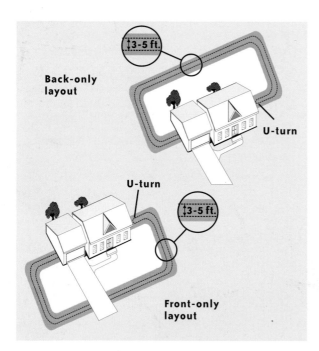

A front- or back-only layout requires a doubled loop of wire to complete the boundary circuit. Starting at the transmitter, the wire encircles the containment area and then doubles back, maintaining a 3- to 5-ft. space (or as directed) between runs to prevent canceling the signal.

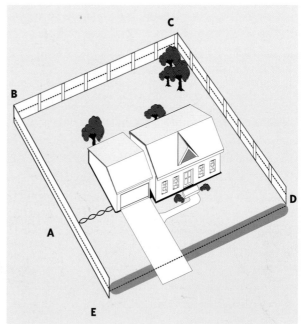

Incorporating a fence into the boundary can help deter your dog from jumping over or digging under the fence. The wire can be fastened directly to the fence and/or can be buried in front of the fence. Burial allows you to protect gate openings. Run wires from the transmitter to A, A to B, B to C, C to D, D to E, E to A, and then twist wire from A to transmitter.

Plan the layout of the boundary wire. With a
100-ft. tape measure to determine the total
wire run. Factor in extra length for twisted
sections and for making adjustments. O
wire, if necessary. Tip: Use the bounda
with the kit to temporarily mark the
points of the wire route.

D:
T:

olding the wire at the end of a loop
linear foot (or as recommended).

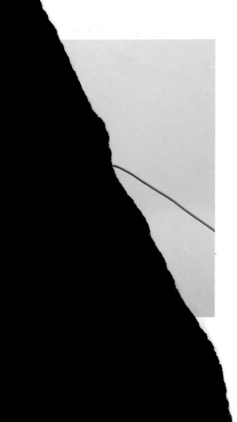

Fasten the boundary wire to fences, as directed by the manufacturer. Use staples for wood fences and plastic zip ties for metal fences (or simply weave the wire through chain link mesh). To protect gate openings, bury the wire in the ground in front of the opening.

Position the boundary flags using the collar to find the inside edge of the warning zone. Move toward the boundary until the collar beeps (warning signal) and place a flag at that location. Place a flag every 10 ft. (or as directed) over the entire boundary area. Fit the collar to your pet as directed to begin the training. After the training period, remove flags (follow manufacturer instructions).

Accessories

DOGS COME WITH A NUMBER OF ACCESSORIES; SOME ARE NECESSARY, SOME ARE NOT. BUT IT DOESN'T TAKE long for a house to fill up with myriad doggy paraphernalia. Even if you're frugal, you'll end up with a head-spinning collection of dog stuff. Most of the accessories we will be building in this chapter fall into the want-to-have category. These accessories enhance our dogs' lives, and sometimes ours as well.

Feeding stations are a must-have; you can choose regular bowls made of ceramic or stainless steel and put them in the predetermined feeding area of a kitchen or mud room. This usually works well, especially for smaller dogs. Or you can enhance your large or geriatric dog's eating experience with the gift of comfort and build him a raised feeding station. Ramps help older dogs get into cars, and anywhere else they would otherwise need to be lifted, so that you don't throw out your back. Dog doors give dogs easy access to fenced-in yards and save you the trouble of getting up every time your dog wants to go in or out. Toy chests, of course, keep all those doggy playthings contained in one place. They are invaluable for quick pickups when unannounced guests knock on your door. And grooming stations keep all those brushes, shampoo bottles, and nail clippers—everything you need to keep your dog looking fabulous and smelling un-dog-like—organized and easily accessible. So grab your tool belt and let's get started!

Dog Bowls

...e remarkably varied. You can get bowls made of plastic, ceramic, or stainless steel. Each
... pitfalls. Plastic can be chewed, and may harbor bacteria; ceramic can break and get jagged
...el is light and can get moved around easily by an enthusiastic eater. Wide, shallow bowls are
...s with pushed-in faces; narrow, deep bowls allow the fur of long-eared, hairy-faced dogs to
...he bowl and stay neat and clean.

...bowls abound. Some keep dogs from snarfing down their food, a behavior that can lead to bloat,
...ening stomach condition. Some are continuous feeders that fill a dog's bowl automatically. And some
...d.

...ecially useful for large and geriatric dogs, elevated bowls alleviate strains caused by leaning down to eat,
...od posture, reduce stomach and other digestive disorders, and can help long-eared, hairy-faced dogs stay
...r and cleaner. Plus raised bowls are out of reach of rodents, ants, and dirt. No matter your dog's size, there
...n optimum eating height: six inches below a large dog's withers, or shoulders; and 4 inches below a small
...og's withers.

Dog Diets

The variety of dog foods available can accommodate any budget and any special diet regimens. Dry foods that contain fillers, such as corn and other grains, preservatives, and dyes tend to be the most affordable but also the least healthy of the dog diets. Dry foods made of human-grade meat and fresh fruits and vegetables can be pricy, but they're healthier than the less expensive brands.

Food specially geared to arthritic dogs; vegetarian dogs; overweight dogs; allergy-prone dogs; and young, medium-aged, and old dogs are just a sample of how canine nutritionists have pinpointed the curative aspects of doggy diets.

Dry kibble and canned food are not your only commercial choices either. Today you can find fresh raw food, freeze-dried raw food, organic foods, and meals that mimic our own human dinners. Some people even choose to cook for their dogs. It's important for these canine chefs to have some sort of direction from a veterinarian to ensure a balanced diet for their dogs.

The meats are more varied now than ever before as well. The typical meats like chicken and beef are still available, but more exotic meats can be had as well. You can feed your dog lamb, fish, bison, venison, and duck. Even more exotics like brushtail and kangaroo can be had for the particularly picky pooch.

And we can't forget about water. All dogs need a ready supply of clean, fresh water, just like their owners.

Tools, Materials & Cutting List

- Measuring tape
- Straightedge guide
- Speed square
- Clamps
- Drill with countersink piloting bit and ³⁄₈" twist bit
- Circular saw
- Jigsaw with scrolling blade
- Miter saw
- Hammer
- Sandpaper and sanding block
- Drum sander attachment for power drill

- Compass
- (1) ¾" × 12" × 48" plywood panel
- (1) 1" × 8 ft. outside corner molding strip
- (1) 1" × 2" × 4' pine
- (4) 1 × 3" Gripper pads
- (24) 2" wood screws
- ¾" brad nails
- Polyurethane stain/finish or paint
- (2) Circular dog food/ water bowls, tapered with top diameter greater than base diameter

Key	Description	Dimension	Pcs.	Material
A	Platform	¾ × 12 × 24"	1	¾" plywood
B	Legs	¾ × 3 × 12"	4	¾" plywood
C	Brace leg	1 × 2 × 22½"	2	1 × 2 × 4' pine
D	Platform trim long	24"	2	8 × 1" corner molding
E	Platform trim short	12"	2	8 × 1" corner molding

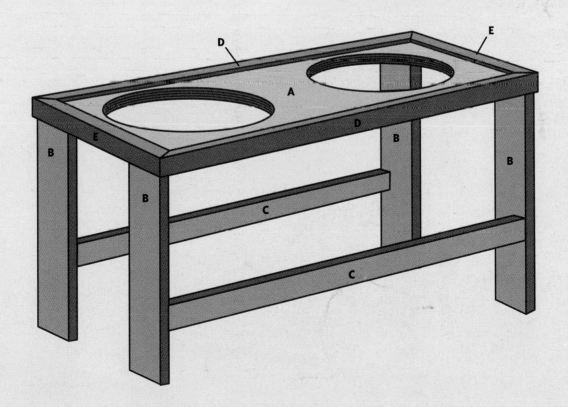

How to Build a Raised Dog Bowl

1

Identify and mark the centers of the bowl locations by measuring 6" in from the outside edge and 6" up from the front edge, using the speed square as a guide.

PREPARING THE PLATFORM

Cut the four 3 × 12" legs from the end of the ¾ × 12 × 48" panel using a circular saw. A straightedge guide and speed square are required to ensure straight cuts at the correct angle. Set the legs aside for sanding.

Cut the platform so it measures approximately 24 × 12". Using the speed square, identify the centers of the bowl locations by measuring and marking 6" in from the outside edge and up 6" from the front edge. The intersections of these marks represent the bowl centers (photo 1). Now measure the diameter of the dog bowl at the base and the top lip. The average of these diameter measurements will be used as the hole cutout diameter for the bowls. Divide the diameter by two to determine the cutout radius. Adjust the compass span to this radius value. Draw a circle on the platform referencing the bowl center locations, using a compass, adjusted to the cutout radius (photo 2).

2

Using a compass, draw a circle sized for your dog bowls on the platform, referencing the bowl center locations.

Make circular cutouts for the dog bowls using a jigsaw. Drill starter holes in the waste area.

Drill a ⅜" hole in the platform inside of each of the compass-drawn circles. Cut out the circular sections using a jigsaw with a scroll blade. Begin the cuts at the drilled ⅜" holes. Clean up and smooth the cutout section of the platform with a drill-attached drum sander (photo 3).

ATTACHING THE LEGS
Sand the four legs to a smooth texture.

If a stain and/or clear finish is to be applied, sand all wood with 220-grit sandpaper for the best appearance.

For latex paint, sanding to a medium texture is adequate. Place the platform upside down on the work bench. Position the legs at each of the four corners of the platform. The narrow section of each leg should be facing front to back. Mark the leg positions on the platform with a pencil. Now orient the platform on its side, the short length on the bench, and position the lower legs at the marked locations. Drill two pilot holes from the platform into each of the two legs keeping the legs in position with clamps or an extra hand (photo 4). Drive two 2" wood screws from the top of the platform into the legs. Flip the platform over and repeat these steps.

Cut the 1 × 2 into two 22" lengths. Sand the wood to the desired texture. These pieces will act as braces for the two front and back legs. Orient the platform (with joined legs) upside down again. Fasten the 1 × 2s to the legs at the approximate middle of the leg span (centered at about 6" up from the platform). A bar clamp is useful to hold the legs together, securing the 1 × 2 for fastening. The long face should be vertical (photo 5). Use one wood screw to join each leg to its respective 1 × 2, piloting the holes as before.

INSTALLING TRIM

Hand cut two lengths of corner trim, mitering to 45°. The inside (short side) dimension should be 24". Cut two additional lengths of trim in the same manner to 12" inside. Fasten the trim pieces to the platform outer edges using brad nails (photo 6). Again, a clamp is a useful assistant for this fastening task.

FINISHING

Sand the top of the platform and the trim to the desired texture. Paint, stain, or finish the wood surfaces as desired. A gloss finish is recommended for easier cleanup of the inevitable spills, splatters, and overflow.

The wood trim installed above will act as spill containment if the bowls form a seal with the cutout holes. This can be facilitated by installing a ¼" strip of closed-foam weather strip around the bowl cutouts.

Apply self-adhesive gripper pads to the bottoms of the legs if the raised bowls are to be placed on a hard floor surface.

Attach the platform to the legs. Drill two pilot holes from the platform into each of the two legs.

Attach the spreaders to the legs at the middle of the leg span, centered at 6 ¾" up from the platform, using wood screws. Use bar clamps to secure the parts together while fastening.

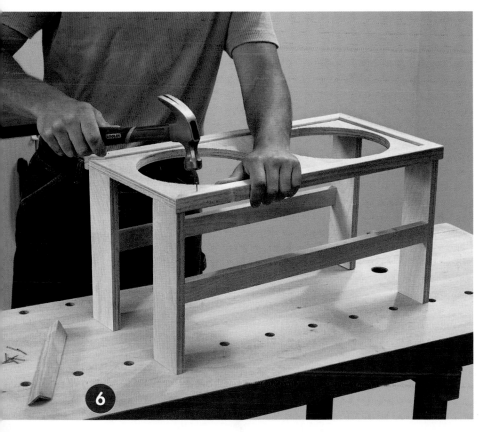

Fasten the mitered trim pieces to frame the platform, using ¾" brads.

Dog Ramp

Is your dog elderly? Is he a large dog? Is he a small dog? Does he have an injury? Does he have difficulty using the stairs? If you answered yes to any of these questions, then your dog would benefit from a ramp. Ramps become useful when you're loading your dog into a vehicle, when your dog wants to lay in your bed or on your sofa (only if allowed!)—any time a dog needs to get to a higher or lower place. The benefit to you is peace of mind that your dog isn't injuring himself every time he jumps onto or off of something, and you save your back from strain or injury.

You want to ensure the ramp you build has good footing, including a nonslip surface, and is stable. Your dog should feel completely confident when walking up and down the ramp.

Tools, Materials & Cutting List

- Measuring tape
- Circular saw
- Jigsaw
- Cutting guide
- Handsaw
- Drill/driver with bits
- ⅜" countersink bit
- Hammer
- Utility knife
- Carpet tacks
- Carpet adhesive
- Indoor/outdoor carpet runner
- 1¼" and 2" wood screws
- Exterior wood glue
- (2) 1 × 4" × 8' oak
- (1) 1 × 2" × 10' oak
- (1) ¾ × 14" × 6' exterior plywood

Key	Part	Dimensions	Pcs.	Material
A	Rail	¾ × 3½ × 66"	2	Oak
B	Deck	¾ × 14 × 60"	1	Exterior plywood
C	Support	¾ × 1½ × 56"	2	Oak
D	Carpet runner	14 × 66"	1	Indoor / outdoor carpet

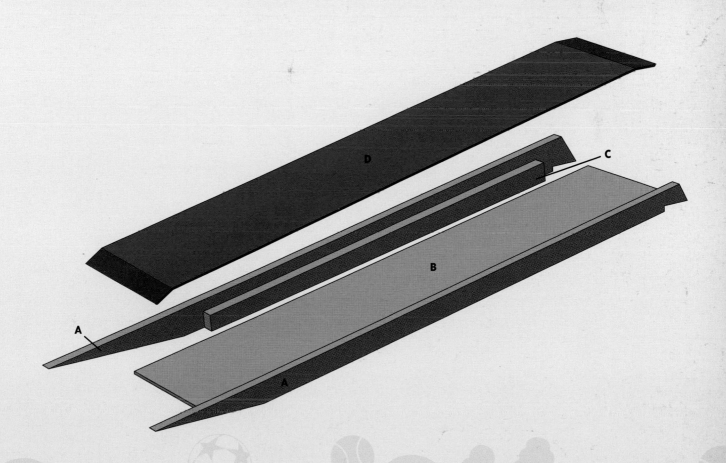

Sizing Your Ramp

To size your ramp, measure from the ground to the top surface of whatever it is you want to give your dog easy access to—a sofa, bed, or vehicle, for instance. This ramp is sized to fit a midsize SUV with a 30" height to the cargo area (the Cutlist on page 93 is designed for 30" of elevation). This creates a slope of 27°, which is slightly shallower than 30°, the maximum slope you should use. At 66", the ramp is about as long as it can be for stowing in the vehicle. See the ramp chart to find the overall length of the ramp you should build for varying heights (if you are a geometry whiz you can calculate the exact size you'll need for a 30° slope).

Required ramp size:

Bumper height (top)	Overall ramp length
Up to 20"	44"
20 to 22"	49"
22 to 24"	53"
24 to 26"	58"
26 to 28"	62"
28 to 30"	66"
30 to 32"	72"
32 to 34"	74"
34 to 36"	81"

Dogs and Cars

DO NOT allow your dog to roam free in your car, especially near open windows. As everyone knows, dogs love to hang their heads out of windows. Failing to prevent them from doing so is very dangerous to your pet and can be a major distraction to the driver.

DO restrain your dog with a car safety belt or crate him securely in the cargo area. Make sure your pets have plenty of ventilation, access to water, and are NEVER left unattended in your vehicle.

How to Make a Dog Ramp

Use a cutting guide and a circular saw or a table saw to make straight cuts for the plywood ramp deck.

CUT THE PARTS

Cut the rails to length according to the size chart on page 94. Use a strong, durable lumber such as dimensional red oak 1 × 4. Then rip-cut the ramp deck to width using a circular saw, a straightedge guide, or a table saw (photo 1). The deck should be 6" shorter than the total rail length. If your bumper is constructed so you can hook the rails of the ramp to it, cut a bird's mouth notch at the end of each rail to fit onto the bumper. Otherwise, you can leave the ends square cut and plan on using your foot or a weight to secure the ramp at the ground when your dog Is on It. Cut out the notches (photo 2).

The ramp will be most stable if you cut the other ends (the ones that rest on the ground) so they are parallel to the ground when the ramp is in position. You can use math to calculate this, or simply clamp a rail to your workbench at your vehicle's bumper height and draw a cutting line at the bottom that's parallel to the floor. Trim off this end of each rail.

Cut the ramp deck support strips from 1 × 2 stock (oak) so they are at least 4" shorter than the ramp deck length.

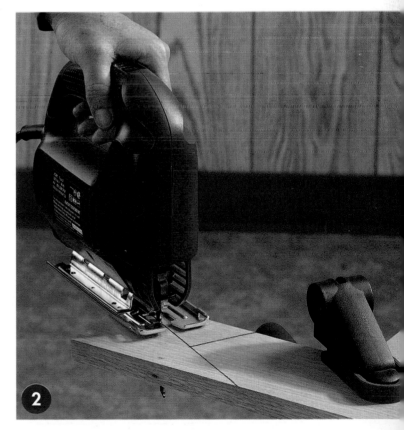

Use a Jigsaw to carefully cut the bird's mouth cutouts at the ends of the rail, where they will hook onto your vehicle.

Drill countersunk pilot holes and fasten the supports to the rails with 1¼" screws.

ASSEMBLE THE RAMP

Glue the ramp deck supports flush with the bottom edges of the rails and clamp in place, keeping them clear of any notches you cut for the bumper. Fasten the supports to the rails, using 1¼" screws driven every 6" into countersunk pilot holes (photo 3).

Next, glue the ramp deck to the supports and fasten it with 2" screws spaced every 8" and driven into countersunk pilot holes (photo 4). The ramp deck should also stop clear of any top notches, and make sure it does not extend past the bottom edges of the rails (trim the deck length if it does).

If you want to get fancy, fill screw countersinks with wood putty and sand smooth when dry. Finish the rails and deck underside as desired (do not apply finish to the top surface of the deck).

You could apply non-skid strips to the ramp to assist with footing, but your animal will feel much more comfortable (and be more willing to use the ramp) if you cover the deck with carpeting instead (cheap indoor/outdoor carpeting is perfect). Cut the carpeting to fit over the deck and tightly between the rails. Overhang each end of the deck. Remove the carpet and spread carpet adhesive or exterior glue onto the deck. Replace the carpet and press it into the adhesive (photo 5). Wrap the overhang carpeting around the ramp deck and secure to the underside with carpet tacks.

Screw and glue the rails to the ramp with 2" screws driven into countersunk pilot holes and spaced at 8" intervals.

5

Secure the carpet to the deck with an exterior-rated glue or adhesive.

Alternative Joinery

If you have a router or a table saw with a dado blade, you can cut dado grooves for the ramp deck and eliminate the ramp deck supports.

- Cut ¾" wide, ⅜" deep grooves in the rails at the position of the ramp.
- Glue and screw the rails to the ramp with countersunk screws spaced 8".

Dog Door

Dog doors are available in a variety of styles, colors, materials, and mechanisms. Install one and your dog can go outside whenever he wishes with nary a lift of a finger from you. But don't even consider installing a dog door to the outdoors if you don't have a securely fenced-in yard. To avoid the potential for someone opening the gate in your yard and unintentionally letting your dog loose, locked gates are also a must.

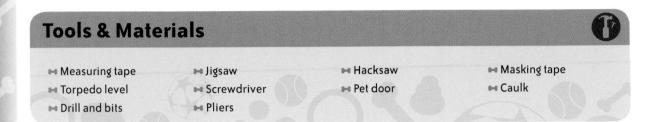

Tools & Materials

- Measuring tape
- Torpedo level
- Drill and bits
- Jigsaw
- Screwdriver
- Pliers
- Hacksaw
- Pet door
- Masking tape
- Caulk

Hard Plastic or Vinyl Flap

Dog doors have either a hard plastic or a soft vinyl flap. There are pros and cons to each. Hard plastic is noisier than vinyl and a dog may have a more difficult time getting used to it. Hard plastic flaps can weather the heat better, though; the vinyl flaps can become deformed and fail to seal properly. Although hard plastic flaps will last longer than the vinyl ones, you can buy replacement vinyl flaps from most dog door manufacturers.

Electronic or Manual Door

One of your biggest decisions when faced with the plethora of dog door styles will be choosing between the electronic and the manual dog door. If cost is a factor, you're going to lean toward the manual; if security is your greatest concern, then your best bet is the electronic door.

How to Determine Your Dog Door's Size

If yours Is a multi-pet household, size the dog door so that your largest pet can access it easily. If you have a puppy and can determine how large he will grow, buy a door that will accommodate his adult size. You can build a ramp to help your puppy reach the door (see Dog Ramp on page 92). The rule of thumb in sizing a dog door is to have at least a 1-inch clearance from side to side, from top of the shoulders, and from below the chest.

- Measure your dog across the shoulders and add 2 inches to determine the minimum opening width of your dog door.
- Measure your dog from the chest (or the lowest part of his torso) to the top of the shoulders and add 2 inches to determine the minimum opening height of your dog door.
- Measure your dog from the floor to the bottom of the chest or stomach, whichever is lower, and subtract 1 to 2 inches to determine the rise, or bottom opening, of the door.

To double-check your measurements, you can outline the door to size on a piece of cardboard, cut out the opening, and have your dog do a test run through the "door." If he's reluctant to go through your dog door prototype, try some of the techniques described in the Dog Door Training section.

Electronic Door Training Tip

Some dogs are frightened at first by the sound emitted by the electronic door when it's activated. To get your dog used to the door, deactivate the electronics for the first few days. Then slowly introduce your dog to the fully activated door with a lot of cheers and treats on hand.

The electronic door is made of hard plastic or Plexiglas, and it responds to an infrared signal from what is called a key that is attached to the dog's collar. It can emit a hum when activated, which is disconcerting to some dogs at first. Electronic doors are more secure and more weatherproof than the manual doors. When shopping for an electronic dog door, pay attention to the specs; some electronic doors open in only one direction.

Dog Door Training

Some dogs will go through the door right away without a problem, but most need to have some level of introduction or training. It's important that you introduce your dog to this contraption slowly and cheerfully. If you know a friendly dog who already uses a dog door, invite him over. Dogs do learn from each other. Barring a friendly canine teacher, there are some simple techniques that with enough patience are bound to work.

Before you install the flap, take the one item that is most irresistible to your dog and go to the other side of the door. Slowly wave the goody just under your dog's nose and lure him toward you through the door. Give your dog the come command in a cheerful and encouraging manner. If your dog doesn't follow the lure, find another item that is even more irresistible.

Once your dog is stepping through the dog door like it's no big deal, install the flap. Go to the side of the door opposite your dog, pull the flap toward you just a bit, and lure your dog as you did when the door was wide open. Do this a few times so your dog gets used to the feel of the flap against his body, then just call your dog to go through the door, flap and all. Any time you hit a snag, go back to the last point your dog behaved reliably, and train slowly from there.

How to Install a Pet Door

MARK CUTOUT ON DOOR

Measure the largest animal that will be using your door and purchase a pet door that is a little larger. Measure a dog's breadth across the shoulders and depth between shoulder tops and bottom of rib cage (see page 29).

Center the template that comes with the pet door on the lower middle of the human door. The ideal height of a dog door top is about 2" above the standing dog's shoulders. For structural reasons, the cutout should not fall below 3" from the bottom of the human door (photo 1).

Center the template with a measuring tape. Level with a torpedo level, tape in place, and draw cutout lines and bolt hole locations. Remove the template.

DRILL BOLT HOLES AND CUT OPENING IN DOOR

Drill the prescribed bolt holes. Next, drill starter holes just inside the corners of the cutout rectangle for the jigsaw blade.

If the door is metal, pound a dimple into the surface at each hole location with a nail, and then drill through

with progressively larger bits until you can fit your saw blade through.

Cut along the side and bottom cutout lines with a jigsaw. Cut the top side last. Tape the cutout in the door as you go to support it, and to keep it from splintering or tearing (photo 2).

PREPARE OPENING IN A PANEL DOOR

If the pet door straddles a rail and a recessed panel or panels, you'll need to even out the opening so the door has a flat installation surface. Measure the depth of the panel relative to the rails with a ruler and a board held across the rails of the door. Rip-cut strips of blocking to this thickness out of 3/4"-thick stock.

Measure and cut the blocking to length to fill low panel areas and glue pieces of blocking around the opening. Put blocking on each side of the opening for pet doors with both an interior and an exterior trim kit (photo 3).

When set, use the door template to re-drill bolt holes. Caulk any gaps between door and framing.

PREPARE OPENING FOR HOLLOW DOOR

A hollow interior door is just that: hollow. Though many have ribbed cardboard or insulating material inside, these fillers have no structural integrity. Use the following method to provide support for the door after cutting the hole in the door.

Rip-cut blocking from 2 × 6 framing lumber to span the gap between the inner and outer skins of the door. Cut to length, glue, and clamp the blocking in place around the perimeter of the hole.

Drill the bolt holes and proceed with the installation.

ATTACH THE PET DOOR

Insert inside and outside door components and bolt together through bolt holes (photo 4). Trim bolts and attach flap according to manufacturer's instructions. The exact installation requirements will vary.

If needed, tape the pet door flap up until your pet becomes accustomed to using the door.

For a dog, the top of the pet door should slightly exceed the dog's full-grown height measured at the shoulders. To keep your human door sturdy, be careful not to cut within 3" of the bottom.

A jigsaw works well for cutting the door hole. Drill starter holes at the corners. Use a metal-cutting blade for an aluminum storm door.

2

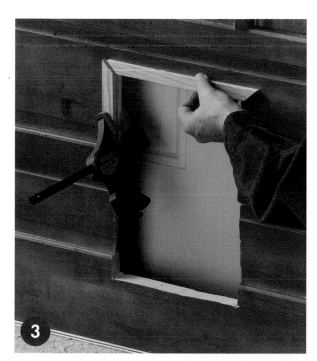

3

Frame the opening with blocking (in frame-and-panel doors); then, fashion and secure frames around the opening to create a flat surface for your pet door.

4

Pet door frames usually come in two pieces that sandwich the cutout panel and bolt together through holes you've drilled in the human door.

Toy Chest

Just as with children's toys, dog toys can quickly take over your house. Many a twisted ankle has a dog toy to blame. And for those of us who like to keep a neat home, dog toys scattered all over the house is just plain unacceptable. But what options do we have? Piling dog toys in a corner is unsightly, and tossing them into the yard just moves the problem to the outdoors. Well, just as with children, a toy chest is the answer.

This easy-to-build doggy toy chest can be personalized in many different ways such as painting your dog's name on it or stenciling dog symbols, such as bones and paws, on it—just to give you a couple of ideas. Be creative, and when you're finished you'll have a unique and attractive addition to your home and a tidier house to boot.

Tools, Materials & Cutting List

- Measuring tape
- Circular saw
- Straightedge
- Clamps
- N95-rated dust mask
- Jigsaw
- Bar clamps (4)
- Drill with standard bits and countersink bit
- Hammer
- Nail set
- Putty knife
- Miter saw
- 150-grit sandpaper and sanding block
- Wood glue
- 1 sheet 4 × 8' (or 4 × 4' half sheet, if available) ¾" MDF
- 6d and 3d finish nails
- Premixed all-purpose drywall joint compound
- Rag
- Solvent-based primer/sealer
- Paintbrushes
- Paint
- (1) 8' poplar 1 × 4
- Paintable wood putty
- 1¼" wood screws

Key	Part	Dimensions	Pcs.	Material
A	Front/back box panel	¾ × 24 × 14"	2	MDF
B	Side box panel	¾ × 10½ × 14"	2	MDF
C	Bottom box panel	¾ × 12 × 24"	1	MDF
D	Base trim	¾ × 2½" × cut to fit	4	1 × 4
E	Handle	¾ × 2¼ × 6"	2	1 × 4

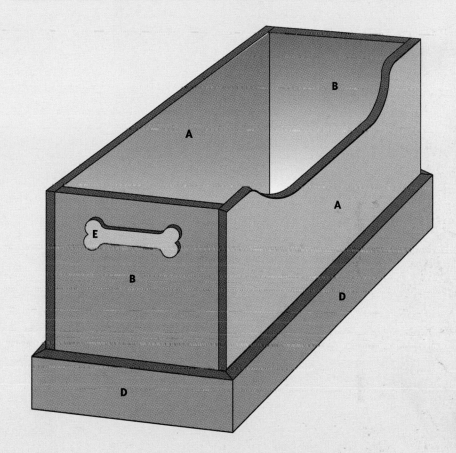

SCALE: GRID = 1"

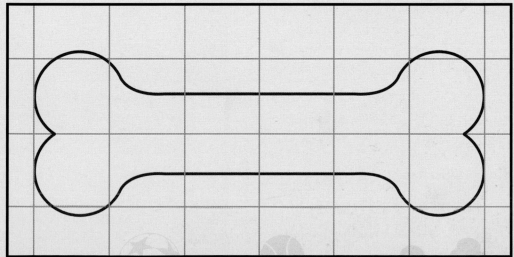

How to Build a Toy Chest

Cut one of the box panels with a circular saw and straightedge guide.

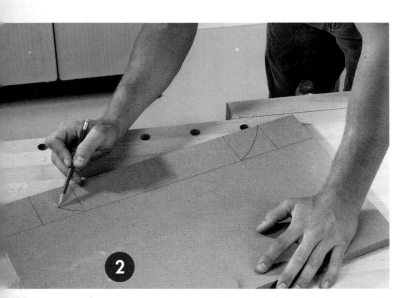

Plot out the profile for the top edge of the front panel. Cut out the profile along the cutting line with a jigsaw.

MDF

Cutting MDF creates a lot of fine airborne dust. It's a good idea to make all cuts outdoors and wear an N95-rated dust mask for all cutting and sanding work.

CUT THE BOX PANELS

The front, back, side, and bottom panels of the toy box are made with ¾" MDF (medium-density fiberboard). MDF cuts easily and cleanly with a circular saw, but it's important to use a straightedge guide to ensure straight cuts; the relatively soft fiberboard material makes it easy for the saw blade to drift away from the cutting line when there's no guide in place. Cutting also creates lots of dust, so wear a good dust mask.

Mark the panels for cutting using the clean factory edges of the MDF sheet for as many finished edges as possible. This reduces the number of cuts needed and ensures straight edges in the finished product. Cut the panels to size.

MAKE THE FRONT-PANEL CUTOUT

The cutout in the front panel of the box makes it easier for a dog to root around in the chest in search of his favorite toy. You can make the cutout as shallow or as deep as you like, depending on the size of your dog, or you can omit the cutout, if desired.

As shown here, the cutout is 3" deep and starts 3" from each end of the front panel. To mark the cutout, draw a line 3" down from and parallel to the top edge of the front panel. Then mark the two starting points along the top edge 3" in from the side edges of the panel.

On the parallel line, mark two end points, each 6" in from the side edges of the panel. Connect each pair of starting and end points with a straight line. This will create a 45° angle between the parallel line and the panel's top edge. Using the straight lines as a guide, soften the corners slightly to create graceful curves at the corners of the cutout (photo 2). Fine-tune the curves as needed until both sides appear identical to the eye.

Make the cutout with a jigsaw and a fine-tooth blade recommended for detailed cuts in MDF.

ASSEMBLE THE CHEST BOX

Lightly sand both faces of each box panel using 150-grit sandpaper and a sanding block. MDF panels are sanded at the factory and are smooth enough to paint, but a light scuff sanding helps glue and primer adhere to the smooth surfaces. Sand only the faces, not the edges, being especially careful not to round over any of the mating edges where panels will be joined together. Vacuum and wipe the panels thoroughly to remove all the dust.

Prime the side edges of the side panels by applying a very thin coat of wood glue, essentially massaging the glue into the wood. This priming coat is needed to prevent the porous edge material from absorbing too much of the final glue application, creating a weak joint. Wait about 15 minutes for the prime coat of glue to dry, then apply an ordinary amount of glue to the same edges, and assemble the box so the front and back panels fit over the ends of the side panels.

Make sure the outside faces of the side panels are flush with the ends of the front and back panels and that all top and bottom edges are flush with one another. Clamp the parts together with bar clamps. Check the inside corners of the box with a square to make sure the entire assembly is square.

Drill pilot holes through the front and back panels and into the edges of the side panels, and fasten the parts together with 6d finish nails. Keep the outer nails at least 2" away from the top and bottom edges (to prevent splitting of the side panels), and space three more nails evenly in between. Use a nail set to drive the nails slightly below the surface of the panel faces. Let the glue dry overnight, then remove the clamps.

Install the bottom panel using the same techniques, priming the bottom edges of the side, front, and back panels, as before, and gluing and fastening the bottom panel over the edges of the other panels (photo 3). Again, keep the outer nails at least 2" from the panel corners.

PREPARE THE BOX EDGES

As with the glue priming, it's a good idea to cover the bare edges of MDF to ensure a smooth finish without excessive painting. Coat the bare edges with drywall joint compound, which is available in small and large buckets. Buy the smallest size you can find, since you'll use very little on this project.

Before coating the edges with compound, smooth and slightly round over the corners of the top panel edges and along the side corners of the box with 150-grit sandpaper.

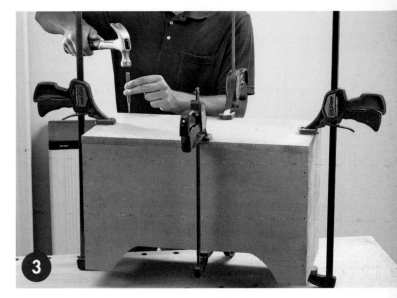

Assemble the chest panels. Clamp together and fasten with finish nails driven through pilot holes. Clamp the bottom panel to the side, front, and back panels with bar clamps.

Apply joint compound to the exposed edges of the chest panels and to nail holes using your index finger. Sand compound smooth after it dries.

There's no need to sand or add compound to the bottom panel, as it will be covered by the base trim. Remove all sanding dust with a rag.

Apply a coat of primer to the bare wood. Primer helps paint bond to wood and limits bleedthrough.

Create a paper template for the bone cutout. Tape the template to a 1" × 4" workpiece and trace cutting lines. Cut the bone out using a jigsaw or scroll saw.

Apply the compound to the top edges of the side, front, and back panels, using your finger to spread the compound into a smooth, even layer (photo 4). Clean up any spillage with a putty knife and a rag. Let the edges dry completely.

Sand the compound lightly with 150-grit sandpaper so it is perfectly smooth and transitions seamlessly into the surrounding bare surfaces. Also sand any rough areas of spillage residue; it's ok if the whiteness of the compound remains, as long as the surface is smooth.

PRIME AND PAINT THE CHEST

Clean the chest to remove all sanding dust. Prime all surfaces with a solvent-based primer (don't use water-based primer, which can make the wood swell, creating a rough surface), following the manufacturer's directions (photo 5). Let the primer dry completely, as directed.

Paint the chest with two or more top coats of the water-based (latex) or oil-based paint of your choice (once primed, it's ok to use water-based paint on MDF).

CREATE THE CHEST HANDLES

The bone-shaped handles on the chest sides are cut from 6" lengths of 1 × 4 poplar. Cut the two pieces to length using a circular saw and a square or a miter saw to ensure straight cuts.

Create a paper template of the bone shape following the 1" grid template on page 103. Cut out the paper template and tape it in place on one of the 1 × 4 pieces. Trace around the template to form the cutting line (photo 6). Remove the template and complete any lines to bridge across the tape locations. Repeat to mark the remaining 1 × 4.

Cut out the handles with a jigsaw. Sand the cut edges smooth with 150-grit sandpaper. Prime and paint the handles using the top coat color of your choice.

INSTALL THE BASE TRIM

Prime and paint the remaining trim stock of 1 × 4 poplar using the top coat color of your choice.

Cut a 45° miter on one end of the painted trim board using a miter box and backsaw or a power miter saw. Position the board along one side of the chest box with the mitered end at one of the box corners. Mark the board for length by making a mark at the adjacent corner of the box. Cut a 45° miter at the mark.

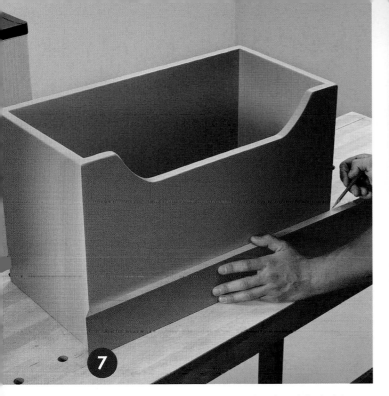

Mark a piece of painted 1" × 4" stock to length by holding it against the chest. Mark and miter cut all four trim pieces in this way.

Fasten the handle to the chest. Secure with a quick release clamp and #6 × 1" screws. Space the countersunk pilot holes evenly along a light pencil line on the inside panel face.

Repeat the process to mark and cut the remaining three trim boards. After cutting each board, hold it in place while you position the next board for marking, fitting the two boards together at the corner joint (photo 7).

Install the boards using 3d finish nails driven through pilot holes, nailing through the trim and into the box panels. Set the nails slightly below the surface with a nail set, being careful not to drive them too far.

Fill the nail holes with wood putty, then touch up the paint at the nail locations and along the corner joints as needed.

INSTALL THE HANDLES

On the outside face of each side panel, draw a light pencil line 3⅝" down from the top edge of the panel, making the line parallel to the top edge. Make a similar line on the inside face of each panel 3⅛" from the top edge.

Position a handle on the outside face so the straight central portion of the handle is on top of the line and the handle is centered from side to side on the chest box. Clamp the handle in place.

Drill three countersunk pilot holes through the inside face of each side panel and into the handle, aligning the holes with the inside pencil line. Fasten the handles with three 1¼" wood screws driven through the inside panel faces (photo 8).

Cover the screw holes with wood putty, and let the putty dry. Touch up the paint on the inside panel faces to hide the putty and pencil lines.

Painting Tips

To make the toy chest's bone handles and base trim stand out, it's best to paint the box with a relatively neutral color, then use a bright or contrasting color for the handles and trim. A neutral color on the box also makes a nice background for painting your dog's name or other custom details on the box panels.

Grooming Station

Regular grooming is an important part of maintaining your dog's health, no matter the length of his fur. And it isn't just fur that is the recipient of a grooming session. Dogs need to have their nails clipped, teeth brushed, and eyes and ears cleaned. If you have a longhaired dog, grooming allows you to check your dog thoroughly for mats, ticks, fleas, lumps, sores—anything that may need attention but would otherwise be hidden by the long fur. Shorthaired dogs benefit from this sort of physical exam as well. Having your own in-house grooming station makes it easy for you to maintain a regular grooming regimen. In most cases weekly grooming is enough, but it's best to groom a longhaired dog daily.

- Stud finder
- Tape measure
- 4' level
- Circular saw and straightedge guide
- Clamps
- Jigsaw and plywood blade
- Utility knife
- Drill and bits
- Hacksaw
- CD or DVD disc
- ¼-sheet (24 × 48") ¾" plywood
- 150-grit sandpaper
- Rubber floor tile and adhesive
- (1) 8' 2 × 2
- (1) 4' 2 × 2
- (2) folding table leg brackets with position lock (for 1½ × 1½" legs)
- 1¼" wood screws
- 3½" coarse-thread wood screws
- ⅝" wood screws
- (1) 1½ × 48" continuous hinge with screws
- (4) wall grid hangers with screws
- (1) 24 × 48" chrome wire wall grid (3" squares or other)
- Wall grid accessories (as desired)

Key	Part	Dimensions	Pcs.	Material
A	Tabletop	¾ × 24 × 42"	1	Plywood
B	Wall cleat	1½ × 1½ × 42"	1	2 × 2
C	Table leg	1½ × 1½ × 32¼"	2	2 × 2

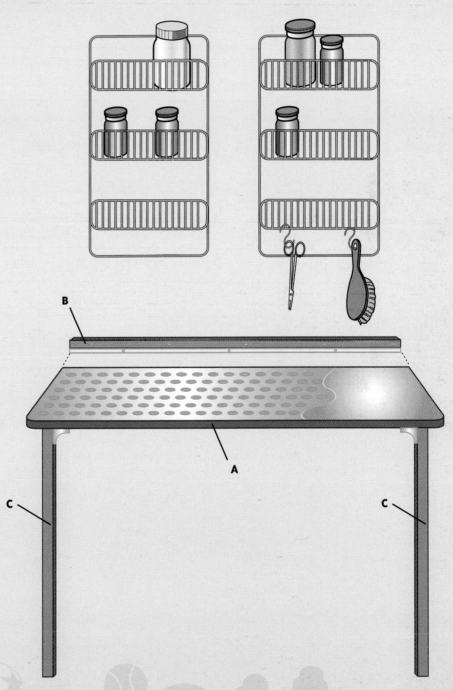

Acclimating your dog to being groomed

The best way to ensure a lifetime if grooming ease is to acclimate your dog to grooming when he's a puppy or as soon as possible after you've adopted an adult dog. This should be a fun and easy process for both you and your dog.

Start by touching your dog all over his body. Be sure to handle his paws, even in between the toes; the fur there may need trimming at some point. Look in your dog's ears and open his mouth. All the while tell your dog how wonderful he's being. If he balks at being touched in a certain place on his body, take note and be extra gentle there the next time you go through this exercise. It won't be long before your dog finds the grooming regimen to be relaxing and enjoyable.

The easiest and most convenient way to ensure proper grooming habits is to have a grooming station in your own home—or yard or garage, depending on climate and setup. Basically all you need to have for a workable grooming station is a laundry tub; table;

nonslip mat; grooming arm, if needed to keep your dog still; and grooming tools.

If you don't have a laundry tub or it isn't big enough to accommodate your dog, you can buy one at your neighborhood home improvement store. The tub should be equipped with a water spray attachment to the faucet. It's a good idea to place a nonskid mat on the floor of the tub.

Grooming tables can be pricey, so we show you how to build one here. If you choose to purchase a grooming arm, keep in mind that most grooming arms attach with a clamp, so make sure the clamp and table top thickness are compatible. If your dog is too large for a table, grooming on the floor will work. You may want to use knee pads, though, and be sure there's a place for the water to drain into.

Now all you need is a wire wall grid to hold the grooming tools and some shelves so you can organize all your shampoos, conditioners, towels, and other paraphernalia.

Grooming Essentials

Brush, comb, rake, shedding tool: The variety is astounding, and you'll find just the right tools for your dog by asking professional groomers or knowledgeable pet store employees.

Shampoo and conditioner: Specialty shampoos are available for many types of skin conditions such as dry skin, itchy allergy-prone skin, flea and tick infestations, and sensitive skin, to name a few.

Nail clipper and styptic powder: The different styles of nail clippers speak to personal preferences—yours, not the dog's. Nail scissors, guillotine styles, and nail grinders are a few of your options. Be careful not to cut your dog's nails to the quick, which can be painful and bleed. If you do, and most of us do at one time or another, use styptic powder (or corn starch) to staunch the bleeding.

Toothbrush and toothpaste: Finger brushes, classic toothbrushes, and flavored toothpaste especially geared to dogs are what you'll need to keep up your dog's oral hygiene. This is more important than you might think. Mouth disease can travel to a dog's heart and create very serious health problems. To combat bad breath alone is a good reason to stay on top of your dog's mouth care.

Clipper, razor, scissors, stripper: The number and types of cutting tools you need will depend on your dog's coat.

Cotton ball, towel, blow-dryer: Cotton balls can be used to clean a dog's eyes, and protect ear canals from water when bathing. You'll want to towel-dry your dog after a bath, and even use a blow-dryer if your dog has long or thick fur. Don't use heat if you're blow-drying your dog.

How to Build a Grooming Station

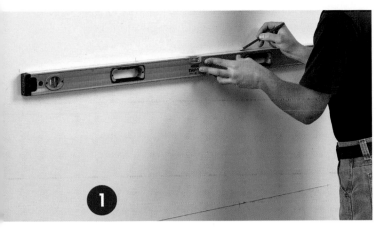

1

Mark the first line at 33" and the second level line at 54" above the floor using a 4-ft. level.

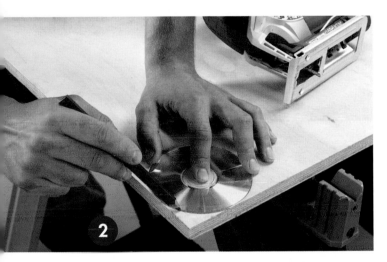

2

Mark the corner cutoff with a CD; tracing along the edge of the disc with a pencil. The plywood top should already be cut to size.

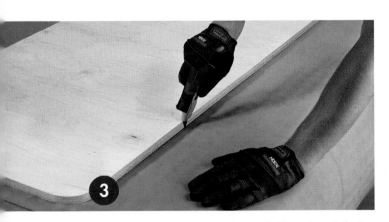

3

Score the rubber tile with a utility knife along the edge of the plywood top.

LOCATE THE STUDS AND MARK LAYOUT LINES

The wall cleat that supports the fixed end of the tabletop must be fastened to two wall studs to ensure long-term durability and provide adequate support for large dogs. You will also fasten the wall grid hangers into the same studs.

Use a stud finder or a hammer and finish nail to locate two adjacent studs in the project area. Make light pencil marks to identify both side edges of each stud.

Mark a layout line for the table cleat using a 4-ft. level. Position the level across both studs and draw a level line at 33" above the floor, or as desired. This is the height of the wall cleat.

Mark a second level line directly above the first at 54" above the floor, or as desired (photo 1). This line represents the bottom edge of the wall grid.

CUT AND SHAPE THE TABLETOP

Cut the tabletop to size using a circular saw and a straightedge guide to ensure straight cuts. As shown, the top measures 24 × 42", but you can adjust the dimensions as needed to suit your dog's size.

The two front corners of the tabletop are rounded for your comfort and your dog's safety. To mark the curve at each corner, place a computer disc (CD or DVD) at the corner so its edge is aligned with both adjacent edges of the plywood. Trace along the disc to mark the curve (photo 2).

Cut the rounded corners with a jigsaw and a fine-tooth blade recommended for smooth cuts in plywood.

Use 150-grit sandpaper to sand the corners of the edges (not the flats of the edges) around the perimeter of the tabletop, rounding over the corners slightly to prevent splinters. If necessary, sand the flats of the edges to remove rough spots that might catch on your clothing but keep this to a minimum; the layers of plywood edges don't sand evenly, due to the alternating grain, and oversanding creates a bumpy surface.

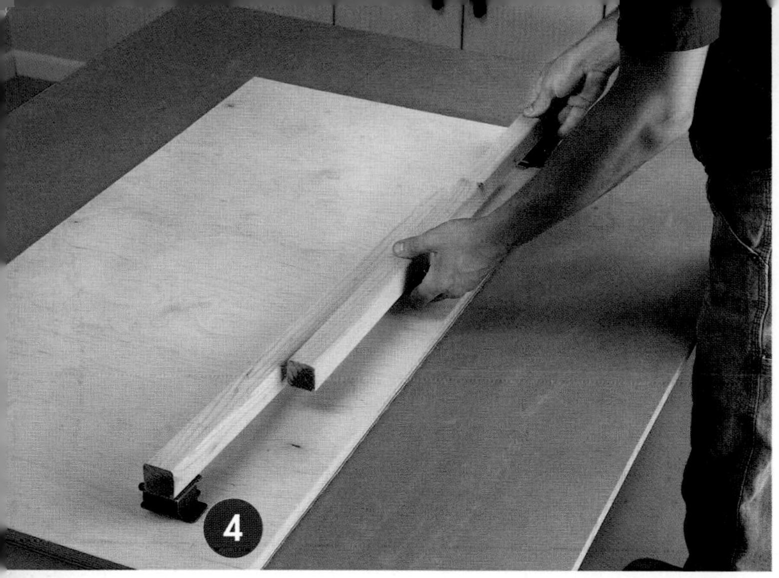

Position the table leg brackets so the legs will fold flat against the tabletop.

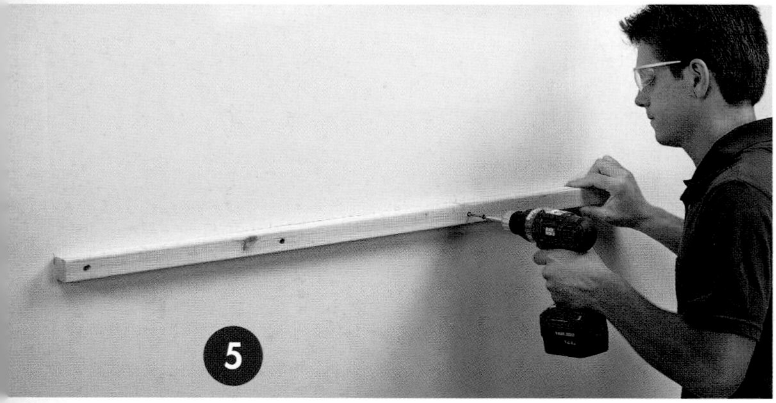

Fasten the 2 × 2 cleat to the wall studs with 3½" screws.

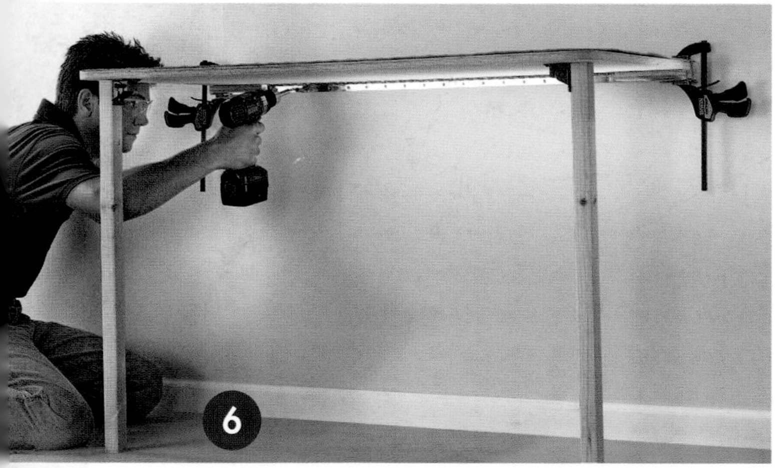

Clamp the tabletop to the cleat. You will need a ¾-thick scrap on the underside of the tabletop, plus a scrap spanning across the scrap and the cleat. You will also need a strip of rubber tile on top of the cleat, plus a scrap spanning over strip and tabletop. Top of plywood should be flush with top of cleat; rubber will be ¼" above cleat.

COVER THE TABLETOP

The top face of the tabletop is covered with rubber to create a washable, nonslip surface. You can use any durable rubber flooring or sheeting material available. The surface shown here is ¼"-thick solid-rubber floor tile sold in 3 × 3-ft. pieces.

Set the rubber tile facedown on your work surface, then position the tabletop facedown over the tile so the plywood is aligned with two of its adjacent edges. Using a utility knife with a new blade, carefully make a score cut into the rubber following the edges of the plywood (photo 3). Remove the plywood and complete the cuts through the full thickness of the tile.

If necessary, use the cutoff piece of the tile to complete the tabletop cover following the same steps to score and cut the remaining piece(s) as needed.

Glue the rubber to the top face of the plywood using the manufacturer's recommended adhesive.

INSTALL THE TABLE LEGS

Cut the 2 × 2 table legs to length using a circular saw (with a square as a guide to ensure straight cuts), a power miter saw, or a miter box and backsaw. You can use standard construction lumber for the leg stock, but standard 2 × 2s often are low quality and not very straight; it might be worth a little extra to buy hardwood, such as poplar or oak.

Mark the locations of the leg brackets onto the bottom face of the tabletop, as appropriate for the bracket you chose. The sides of the legs should be at least 1" in from the side and front edges of the tabletop. To prevent the legs from running into each other when they are folded in, either offset the brackets by about 2" or turn one of the brackets slightly toward the wall side of the table (photo 4).

Drill pilot holes for the brackets and fasten the brackets to the tabletop with ⅝" wood screws. Secure the table legs to the brackets using 1¼" wood screws or as directed by the manufacturer. For stability, the top leg ends should fit tightly against the tabletop when in the open position.

MOUNT THE WALL CLEAT

Cut the 2 × 2 cleat to match the length of the tabletop. Sand the edges to round over the corners slightly to prevent splinters.

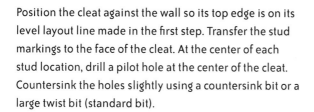

Hang wire baskets from the wall. Two wire baskets should be enough.

Use S-hooks to hang brushes and other tools form the bars of the wire baskets.

Position the cleat against the wall so its top edge is on its level layout line made in the first step. Transfer the stud markings to the face of the cleat. At the center of each stud location, drill a pilot hole at the center of the cleat. Countersink the holes slightly using a countersink bit or a large twist bit (standard bit).

Mount the cleat to the wall with 3½" coarse-thread wood screws making sure the top edge of the cleat is on the level line (photo 5).

INSTALL THE TABLE

Use a hacksaw to cut the continuous hinge (also called piano hinge) to length so it is ½" shorter than the table length.

With the tabletop upside-down on the work bench, position the hinge along the wall-side edge of the tabletop so it is perfectly aligned with the edge of the plywood and the ends are ¼" from the side edges of the plywood. Clamp the hinge in place. Drill a pilot hole for each screw hole in the hinge, being careful not to drill all the way through the plywood top. Fasten the hinge to the plywood using the screws provided.

Open the legs of the table and lock them in position. Fit the wall-side edge of the tabletop against the wall cleat, and use scrap-wood blocks (and strips of the rubber tile) to clamp the tabletop to the cleat. The top face of the plywood should be level with the top edge of the cleat (photo 6).

Drill pilot holes into the cleat, and fasten the hinge to the cleat with the screws provided.

MOUNT THE GRID HANGERS

Metal storage grids typically hang from special brackets that anchor to the wall studs or to heavy-duty hollow wall anchors such as toggle bolts. Use only hangers made specifically for the wall grid you're using.

Position the wall grid on the wall so its bottom edge is on its level layout line made in the first step. Adjust the grid from side to side as needed so the stud centers are aligned with appropriate hanger locations on the grid. Mark the hanger locations onto the wall. It may help to set each hanger in place behind the grid for accurate marking.

Drill pilot holes for the hangers and fasten the hangers to the studs with the screws provided or with 2" coarse-thread wood screws (photo 7).

INSTALL THE GRID AND ACCESSORIES

Because wall grids are designed for both commercial and household applications, manufacturers offer a wide range of shelves, baskets, hooks, hanging bars, and other accessories. All accessories hang right from the grid and are easy to install or reposition as needed.

Secure the grid to the mounting hangers as directed by the manufacturer. Add accessories to the grid as desired. Wire shelves are great for storing towels, and wire baskets work well for bottles of shampoo and other liquids. You can use simple S-hooks to hang brushes, scissors, clippers, leashes, etc. (photo 8).

earing
oose in
eep our
or 3) we can
age. The third

toxic plantlife, other
d training, providing
azards. And some simple
s and waste from projects

e from) your dog.

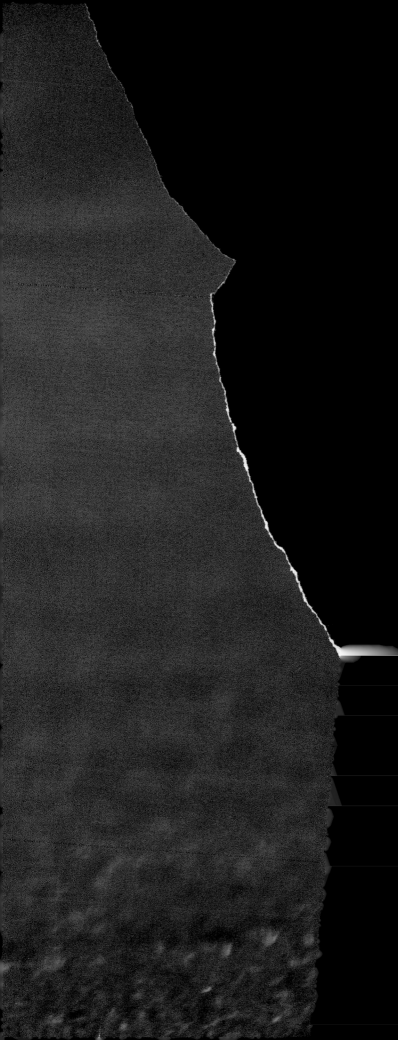

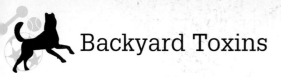

Backyard Toxins

A yard can be booby trapped with a whole slew of toxic (to dogs anyway) plants that look perfectly innocent. Sometimes only certain parts of a plant are poisonous. The hulls of certain nuts can be toxic to dogs, and pits of certain fruits are dangerous as well. Be particularly careful with apricot, peach, and cherry pits as well as the cores of apples.

Be aware that some plants are toxic if eaten. Although many are not deadly and not every part of a plant deemed toxic will actually sicken your dog, it's best to avoid toxic plants altogether. Check with your local nursery to make sure your plant choices are safe. You can find a full list of toxic plants online (see Resources, page 126), but some of the more common ones are:

- Amaryllis
- Autumn Crocus
- Azalea/Rhododendron
- Buckeye
- Castor Bean
- Chrysanthemum
- Cyclamen
- Delphinium
- English Ivy
- Foxglove
- Kalanchoe
- Marijuana
- Mushrooms
- Narcissus
- Oleander
- Peace Lily
- Pothos
- Sago Palm
- Schefflera
- Tulip/Narcissus bulbs
- Yew

Applying mulch around plants is a good idea for many reasons, but you need to choose your mulching material carefully if you have dogs. Some popular mulches, such as cocoa bean, are toxic to dogs.

Pesticides are obviously toxic since their purpose is to kill pests. Look for nontoxic alternatives: Some plants, such as marigolds, can be planted as natural pest repellents; a mixture of soap and water sprayed on flowers will eradicate aphids as will a handful of ladybugs; or you can merely spray aphids off plants with a garden hose or pick them off by hand.

Snail bait is bad for dogs, and yet a perfectly harmless snail eradicator is available: beer. Pour an inch of beer into a shallow container, place it in the garden, and walk away. Snails are attracted to the smell of yeast in beer, and will drown. If you find this too messy, buy bait with iron phosphate as its main active ingredient.

Even organic alternatives to pesticides and fertilizers can be toxic to your dog, especially if consumed in large quantities. Be sure all your gardening material is stored according to manufacturers' recommendations and, this can't be said often enough, safely behind lock and key so your dog has no access to it at all.

Foxtails

Foxtails aren't a toxin, but they can be deadly, and they are so widespread that they've become a real danger to our dogs. A group of grasses with bristles and barbs, foxtails reproduce by catching onto an animal's fur and being transported to another area, dropping off, and taking root. When the grasses become dry and stiff, the barbs can penetrate a dog's nose, mouth, paw—any soft, vulnerable spot. Once in the body, the foxtail can enter the dog's bloodstream and cause a great deal of harm. Usually a visit to a vet and surgery is needed once this has occurred. Do whatever you can to keep foxtails out of your dog-friendly yard!

A meadow foxtail with pollen

Pests & Wildlife

As we build our neighborhoods farther and farther away from the city, we become ever more familiar with the native fauna. Some wildlife move deeper into the wilds to get away from humans, others find a happy coexistence with us. Many of us love to see foxes, hawks, rabbits, raccoons, possum, and yes, even coyotes, skunks, and snakes in our neighborhoods, but how do we protect our dogs from the potential dangers that come with this proximity to the wild?

Many wild animals carry diseases that can be passed on to any animal who comes in contact with them. This becomes even more of a dire situation when a dog catches the diseased wild animal. Any nocturnal animal, such as a raccoon, wandering around during the day or acting bold is likely to be diseased. Stay away. Rabies, distemper, salmonella, and parasites such as ticks, coccidia, giardia, and mange are only a few of the diseases that your dog can acquire from contact with wildlife. If your dog happens to eat or even just taste a toad, she's likely to be exposed to enough toxin from the toad's skin to cause liver damage.

Never forget that dogs are predators; they are hardwired to hunt. When a dog goes after prey, her full attention is on the chase. She doesn't hear you call her, she doesn't notice she's running into the path of a car, she's oblivious to anything that is not prey.

Turtles are very interesting to dogs, but train your dog to keep away from them. Snappers can injure dogs easily, and all varieties are potential carriers of salmonella.

Monitor your dog's food bowl, ensure your garbage cans are tightly lidded, and keep bird feeders out of your dog's territory. Removing these temptations will make your yard far less desirable to wild critters and far safer for your dog.

The Problem of Birdfeeding

You enjoy putting out seeds to lure birds into your yard? Great—but place your birdfeeders out of reach of your dog. The seeds that fall to the ground can become moldy, sickening your dog if she should nibble on them, and they will attract rats, chipmunks, and squirrels. If your dog catches any of these animals and if they have eaten poison bait or are otherwise diseased, your dog will suffer the same.

If she's lucky enough to catch the prey, her instinct, usually, is to kill the animal, but that may not be before she's been bitten or clawed by the prey animal fighting for its life. This is a pretty cruel scenario to imagine your pup participating in, but no dog is immune to this drive. So always have your dog, even if she's an AKC champion, within the safety of a fenced yard or on a leash.

Besides the potential for causing diseases, many uninvited wildlife guests can do bodily harm to your dog. Your first task is to avoid issuing an open invitation to these animals. Unattended dog food bowls, unsealed garbage cans, uncapped chimneys, bird seed under bird feeders—all are temptations that could lure wildlife into your yard. Another way critters are lured into a yard is if it supplies good living and hiding areas. Groundcovers such as ivy are perfect hiding homes for rats. If your yard is wild enough, skunks, raccoons, possum, or even foxes could start housekeeping in your yard.

If you have a medium or large dog, you don't have to worry about birds of prey. But young puppies and small dogs can be whisked away by an attentive raptor. There's not much you can do to prevent this other than be vigilant about supervising your dog when she's outside.

Fencing

To keep coyotes out of your yard, your fence should be at least 6 feet tall and secured to the ground. Better yet, have an additional 12 inches of fencing buried 1 inch underground and angled 90° away from the property to keep any critters from digging under the fence.

Rattlesnakes

Although rare, rattlesnakes do venture into suburbia. The biggest danger, though, is when you're out hiking with your dog. It's so tempting to let your dog off-leash when you're in the wilderness, but don't. On-leash you can keep your dog from stepping in the wrong place or investigating an interesting hole. If you do live in rattlesnake country and do a lot of hiking with your dog, you may want to talk to your vet about the vaccine for rattlesnake bites.

Skunks

Skunks are powerful fighters, but most animals never find this out because a skunk's first defense is to spray. A dog who has been sprayed by a skunk may foam at the mouth, keep her eyes closed, and stink! If you can gently wash out the dog's eyes you can dilute the irritant, but getting rid of the stink is much more difficult. Your best bet is to take your dog to a professional groomer. Even then, a faint skunky smell is likely to shadow your dog for weeks.

Lawn & Garden Care

Dogs don't care how pretty their surroundings are. But the enticing scents in the soil, the cool earth under the sod, and the path that they've trampled in the grass running from here to there—all appeal to the canine aesthetic. Brown spots, dug-up earth, and torn-up grass are the results. But if you put some thought and effort into it, they will mix well. Dog, turf, and garden can co-exist.

Brown Spots

Brown spots in a lawn caused by nitrogen overload are rimmed with dark green. That's because the nitrogen load is far lighter on the edge of the deposit than it is in the center, and at the proper dosage, nitrogen is a great lawn fertilizer. The best way to combat a nitrogen overdose is to turn a hose on the spot. The water dilutes the nitrogen, disarming its damaging effects. This doesn't have to be done right away; you have a couple of hours

Myths

Myth: The pH of urine is what destroys grass.
Truth: The nitrogen in urine is what causes brown spots in grass.
Myth: Changing the dog's diet, adding tomato juice or salt, will eliminate brown spots.
Truth: The only way diet can dilute the nitrogen content in a dog's urine is by adding moisture either by feeding canned food or adding water to dry kibble.

to water down the spot before much damage is done. If you have an automatic irrigation system, you can program your controller to turn on in mid-morning for a couple of minutes. If your dog stays outside all day long, another spritz in mid-afternoon may be warranted

Dogs destroy yards: sometimes actively by digging and tearing around, and sometimes with urine. The best way to manage a canine excavation expert is to direct her to an area in the yard that is hers alone, to dig to her heart's content.

as well. Otherwise, when you see your dog doing her business, be ready with a hose or watering can.

Training your dog to eliminate in only one area of the yard, or taking her on a walk first thing in the morning and as soon as you come home from work (the two times her urine's nitrogen concentration is likely to be the most concentrated) will greatly reduce the occurrence of brown spots in your yard. Training is easiest if you start when your dog is an impressionable pup, but any dog can be redirected to a designated potty area. Once you've determined where this area will be, keep your dog on a leash every time you take her out. Walk her straight to the potty area and use a word or words that your dog can associate with going potty, like "go potty" (you don't need to be poetic about it). When your dog complies, praise her verbally and with a really yummy treat. Do this consistently, and after a few weeks your dog will use only the designated bathroom area to do her business.

Raised planting beds discourage dogs from trampling through your gardens and rooting around. Persistent pups can be further discourage with a low wire fence on the raised bed rails.

Garden Damage

Just as you wouldn't allow your toddler outside without supervision, you shouldn't allow your dog unsupervised in the yard if you want an attractive garden. At first, whether it's the dog or the garden that's new, always be outside with your dog to train her to keep out of certain areas. You'll probably need to redirect your dog's digging, chewing, and trampling urges as well. Fences and tomato cages are great plant protectors. If you decide to fence around your garden, be sure to bury the fence a few inches into the ground so your dog can't dig under it. Raised beds can also help discourage curious canines, as can container gardening.

If you have a dog who likes to pull, put her to work pulling a wagon or garden cart. She'll love having a job and you'll have extra energy for more gardening. Training opportunities abound, so take advantage of this time with your dog.

Tough Turf

Not all grasses are created equal; some are tougher than others and can withstand heavier traffic. Here's a list to help you determine the best turfgrass for your lawn:

Tough Warm Season Grasses	Tough Cool Season Grasses
Kikuyugrarss	Kentucky bluegrass
Bermudagrass	Tall fescue
St. Augustinegrass	Perennial ryegrass
Zoysiagrass	

Be sure to mow high and water your established lawn deeply once a week.

If all else fails, you can opt for a clover ground-cover or to hardscape your yard.

Dog Repellent

If you find your dog loves to pluck, chew, or otherwise desecrate your plants, you can spray a weak mixture of water and cayenne pepper, a distasteful concoction that will cause your dog to lose her taste for homegrown plants.

Dog Damage Remedies

Once you've committed to sharing your home with a dog, you might as well resign yourself to the likelihood that you will have some dog-created damage to your house. Don't despair. In most cases easy fixes and preventive measures are available to help you through these frustrations.

The easiest way to prevent any damage to your home is to limit your dog's access to special areas of the house. This could mean keeping your dog outside while you're away (as long as you have a completely safe, enclosed yard with appropriate shelter), making certain rooms inaccessible either by closing doors or blocking doorways with baby gates, or crating your dog while you're away (as long as you won't be gone for hours on end).

If the idea of denying your dog access to parts of the house is distasteful to you, there are other preventive measures you can take. For instance, you can install a clear vinyl door protector onto your door to protect it from being scratched by your dog in her plea to be let out. Nail caps applied to your dog's nails are another option for protecting your doors, floors, and any other item in your house from being scratched. Of course, your dog's nails should be kept short in the first place. But if none of these preventive measures work for you, you will have to reconcile yourself to learning how to do all sorts of repairs.

Before

After

Dogs can do a surprising amount of damage to doors in their constant quest to answer the call of the wild. Luckily, fixing door scratches is pretty easy.

How to Fix Door Scratches

Tools & Materials

- Utility knife
- Wood filler
- Lights sandpaper
- Rag
- Varnish or paint to match

1

Remove the door and place it on sawhorses. If there are deep gouges in the door, start by using a utility knife to cut out the loose wood chips.

2

Fill the damaged area with wood filler. Use a putty knife to push the filler into the deeper areas. Wait for the filler to dry.

3

For scratches that aren't as deep, use light sandpaper to sand down the edges. Make sure to sand with the grain of the wood.

4

Use a wood filler to fill in the deeper scratches. Wait for the wood filler to dry. When the wood filler is dry, sand it smooth. Wipe away all the dust, and apply paint or varnish to match the rest of the door.

How to Fix Furniture Scratches

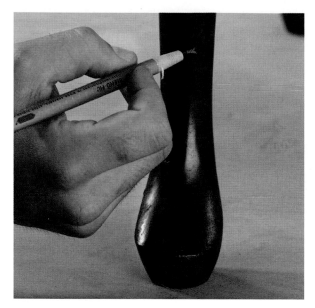

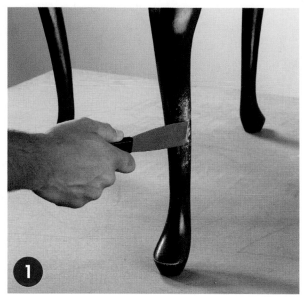

OPTION: For small scratches in wood furniture, simply find a wax blending stick that's the same color as you finish and color the bare wood to blend in (check at woodworkers stores or in woodworking catalogs).

First, if there are any large loose splinters of wood, chisel them out. Sand the smaller splinters on the top and surrounding area of the damaged wood. Use a putty knife to fill the area with the wood filler.

Sand the dried wood filler with a fine-grit (180 to 220) sandpaper until the repaired area is flush with the surrounding wood.

Stain the repaired area, matching the stain to the surrounding wood finish. A combination stain and finish product is easiest to apply, but you may get a better match by coloring the wood filler with stain model paint and dabbing then buffing a small amount of furniture wax.

Common household chemicals that are very dangerous to your dog include: antifreeze, bathroom cleaners, furniture polish, household bleach, and paint strippers.

Our world is filled with chemical solutions to our organic troubles. Many of these chemicals are perfectly safe as long as directions are followed, but most are potentially lethal if swigged straight out of the bottle. Many of these otherwise harsh-smelling chemicals are enhanced with sweet-smelling aromas, making them attractive to the nose. And who has a better nose than a dog? Just as you would baby-proof your home for an inquisitive toddler, you must dog-proof your home for your inquisitive pooch. Store all toxic substances, both indoors and out, behind lock and key.

Many cleaning solutions have toxic chemicals on their ingredients list. Be sure you store them where your dog cannot get to them. Some newer "green" cleaning formulations tout ingredients that are safe for kids and pets. Still, keep these bottles securely out of reach of canine and kid curiosity. You can go the simple route and make your own cleansers out of safe ingredients such as vinegar and water. Some people steam clean their floors and counters as a way to keep chemicals out of the house. You can find many fine books on this topic at book stores and libraries.

Store all chemicals and cleaners on shelves that are well outside your dog's reach. Or better yet, keep them in a locked cabinet.

Photo Credits

Shutterstock, pp. 4, 12, 66-67, 68, 69, 84-85, 94 both, 116, 117, 118 all, 119 bottom

iStockphoto, pp. 10-11, 13, 44-45, 46 top right, 114-115, 125 bottom

Photolibrary, p. 47

Boelke-Art/Getty Images, p. 120

Katewarn Images/Alamy, p. 121 bottom

Sources

List of toxic plants:
http://www.aspca.org/pet-care/poison-control/plants/

Rubber tile to cover tabletop:
www.greatmats.com/products/flec-tile.php

Table leg brackets:
www.rockler.com/ecom7/product_details.cfm?offerings_id=5817

Wall grid panel (2 × 4' chrome grid with 3" squares:
www.gridwall.com/gridwallpanels.html

Wall grid accessories:
www.gridwall.com/basketshelves.htm

Continuous hinge★:
www.cornerhardware.com

★Hinges are available at any home center or online.

Index

A

A-frames, building, 70–71
Agility training, about, 68–69
Agility training equipment,
   building
      A-frames, 70–71
      hoop jumps, 72–73
      weave poles, 74–75

B

Baltic birch, 51
Basic ranch doghouse,
   building, 20–25
Bedding, 13
Beds
      about, 46
      coaxing dog to use, 47
      contemporary, building, 48–53
      denning and, 46
      Mission style, building, 60–65
      nightstand/bed, building,
         54–59
Belt sanders, 8–9
Birdfeeders, 118
Bit drills, 9
Blow-dryers, 110
Brown spots in lawn, 120–121

C

Cars, dogs in, 94
Castle, building custom dog, 14–19
C-clamps, 8–9
Cedar, 7
Circular saws, 8
Clippers, 110
Contemporary dog bed,
   building, 48–53
Cotton balls, 110
Coyotes, 119
Custom dog castle, building, 14–19
Cutting techniques
      general, 8
      MDF, 105
      plywood, 56

D

Denning
      about, 46
      nightstand/bed, building,
         54–59
Diets, 86
Dog bowls, building raised, 86–91
Dog damage remedies
      door scratches, 122–123
      furniture scratches, 124
Dog doors, installing, 99–101
Dog-friendly yards, creating
      about, 116
      birdfeeders in, 118
      foxtail dangers, 117
      lawn & garden care, 120–121
      pests & wildlife, 118–119
      toxins, 117
Doghouses
      advantages, 12
      basic ranch, building, 20–25
      custom dog castle,
         building, 14–19
      green, building, 34–43
      insulated, building, 26–33
      precautions, 13
      sizing, 12–13, 25, 29
      training dog to use, 13
Dog ramps, building, 92–97
Dog repellent, 121
Door scratches, remedying,
   122–123
Dowels, too long, 59
Drilling techniques, 9

E

Electronic doors, 99
Exterior plywood, 7

F

Fencing, 119
Finishes, about, 7
Foxtail dangers, 117
Furniture scratches, remedying, 124

G

Garden damage, 121
Gluing, 9
Grasses, hardy, 121
Grass roofs
      building, 42–43
      maintaining, 40
Green doghouse, building, 34–43
Grooming station
      acclimatizing dogs to
         grooming, 110
      building step-by-step, 111–113
      equipment & materials, 110
      tools, materials & cutting
         list, 109

H

Hardwood, 7
Holes, making, 9
Hoop jumps, building, 72–73
Household chemicals, 125
Hunting instincts, 118–119

I

Insulated doghouse, building,
   26–33
Insulation dangers, 13
Interior plywood, 6
Invisible fences
      about, 76
      advantages and disadvantages
         of, 77
      installing, 79–83
      layout possibilities, 78
      training dog for, 77

J

Jigsaws, 8
Joinery basics, 63

L

Lumber types, 6–7

M

Materials
 Baltic birch, 51
 siding, about, 22
 types, 6–8
MDF (medium-density fiberboard)
 about, 6
 cutting, 105
Mission style bed, building, 60–65

N

Nail clippers, 110
Nightstand/bed, building, 54–59

O

Older dogs, feeding stations for,
 85, 86–91
Oriented-strand board (OSB), 7

P

Painting tips, 107
Paints, about, 7
Palm sanders, 9
Panel types, 6–7
Pests in yards, 118–119
Pet doors, installing, 98–101
Piloting techniques, 9
Plants, toxic, 117
Plugs for wood, 9
Plywood
 Baltic birch, 51
 cutting, 56
 exterior, 7
 interior, 6
 sanded, 7
 types, 6–7
 veneer, 6
Power drills, 9
Power miters, 8
Pressure-treated wood, 7
Putty for wood, 9
PVC (polyvinyl chloride) pipe,
 about, 8

R

Raised dog bowls, building, 86–91
Ranch doghouse, building
 basic, 20–25
Random orbit sanders, 9
Rattlesnakes, 119
Razors, 110
Redwood, 7

S

Sanded plywood, 7
Sanders, 9
Saws, 8
Scaling plans, 25
Scissors, 110
Shampoo and conditioner, 110
Shaping techniques, 8–9
Sheathing, 7
Sheet goods, 6–7
Sizing
 about, 12–13
 adjusting dimensions, 29
 dog doors, 99
 dog ramps, 94
 recalculating plans how-to, 25
Skunks, 119
Softwood construction lumber, 7
Squaring a frame, 9
Strippers, 110
Styptic powder, 110

T

Techniques, 8–9
Toothbrush and toothpaste, 110
Tough turf, 121
Towels, 110
Toxins
 backyard, 117
 household chemicals, 125
Toy chest, building, 102–107

U

Utility doghouse, building, 26–33

V

Veneer plywood, 6

W

Weave poles, building, 74–75
Wildlife in yards, 118–119
Wood
 prepping for finishing, 9
 types, 6–7
Woodworking techniques, 8–9

Y

Yards, creating dog-friendly
 about, 116
 birdfeeders in, 118
 foxtail dangers, 117
 lawn & garden care, 120–121
 pests & wildlife, 118–119
 toxins, 117

Thanks

Special thanks to our dog friends
who appeared in the projects:

Daisy – Shetland Sheepdog
Hades – Miniature Pinscher
Jack – Wire-hair Tox Terrier
Joey – Boxer
Maggie – Brittany Spaniel
Neil – Rhodesian Ridgeback
Sweetums – Terrier/Chihuahua Mix